There is no voice so compelling as the voice of experience. Sandra's story as a breast cancer survivor should be read by every woman facing this daunting giant called "breast cancer." Sandra takes the reader through not only the practical steps of what will likely occur, but also through the range of emotional and spiritual seasons that come as part of the journey. *In the Arms of My Beloved* is a book I highly recommend not only for the cancer patient herself, but also for all those who love her.

Stacey Campbell, *Revival Now! Ministries*
www.beahero.org
www.revivalnow.com

In the Arms of My Beloved, is a compelling, true life story of hope, faith and perseverance leading to the place of triumph over breast cancer. As you read the pages of this book you will be strengthened in your faith and fall more in love with Jesus, knowing that with God all things are possible when you believe in His promises and appropriate His word. This is a must read for everyone who is facing sickness or a personal crisis.

Pastor Lina Gabeli, *Co-pastor of Westwood Community Church*
& Founder of Women of Royal Destiny (WORD) Ministries

"Why do good people suffer?" This has been a question asked of God since the ancient days of Job. While there are many answers to this question one is simply to make a way, to light a path through the darkness that others can follow. Such was the path that Job forged, and countless others that have endured and overcome suffering without losing hope or faith. Another such trailblazer is Sandra Crawford. Sandra shares her journey through the valley of the shadow of death named "cancer" with complete, disarming honesty, and yet each page is filled with life, hope and healing as she finds and invites us into a new depth of relationship with God in the process. For anyone touched by cancer or any other life-threatening disease this book will be a lifeline to hope.

Sara Maynard, *Founder and Director, Redleaf Prayer Ministries*

Throughout her journey with breast cancer, Sandra has refused to stay down or be embittered, but has overcome every challenge with faith, courage and determination. Her inspiring story offers hope and practical wisdom to those who are walking through difficult times, especially when faced with serious or life-threatening illnesses.

Dr. Ruth Demian, *MD*

In candidly telling her story, Sandra Crawford shares valuable lessons we can all learn from, no matter what giants we face in life. As a two-time cancer survivor, I could relate to Sandra's epic journey of seeking and find the source of hope, strength, and courage amidst the darkest of circumstances.

Rosalie Conway, *Two-time Cancer Survivor*

In the Arms of My Beloved

A Journey through Breast Cancer

by

Sandra Crawford

WestBow
PRESS
A DIVISION OF THOMAS NELSON

ISBN: 978-1-4497-6040-3 (sc)
ISBN: 978-1-4497-6041-0 (hc)
ISBN: 978-1-4497-6039-7 (e)
Library of Congress Control Number: 2012913966

WestBow Press books may be ordered through booksellers or by contacting:
WestBow Press
A Division of Thomas Nelson
1663 Liberty Drive
Bloomington, IN 47403
www.westbowpress.com
1-(866) 928-1240

Because of the dynamic nature of the Internet, any web addresses or links contained in this book may have changed since publication and may no longer be valid. The views expressed in this work are solely those of the author and do not necessarily reflect the views of the publisher, and the publisher hereby disclaims any responsibility for them.

Permissions from copyright holders have been given:
Dutch Sheets Ministries
Pastor Henry W. Wright for Be in Health Ministries
Canadian Cancer Society/National Cancer Institute of Canada:
Canadian Cancer Statistics 2006, Toronto, Canada, 2006, ISSN 0835-2976

Unless otherwise noted, Scripture quotations are taken from the NIV of the Holy Bible, New International Version®. NIV®. Copyright © 1973, 1978, 1984, by International Bible Society. Used by permission of Zondervan Publishing House. All rights reserved. Scripture quotations marked "NKJV®" are taken from the New King James Version®. Copyright © 1982 by Thomas Nelson, Inc. Used by permission. All rights reserved.

Cover graphics by Ryan Tsuen based on a painting by Tracy Wong
Author's photo by bopomo pictures   www.bopomo.ca
Back cover photos (background and eagle) by Sandra Crawford

Any people depicted in stock imagery provided by Thinkstock are models, and such images are being used for illustrative purposes only.
Certain stock imagery © Thinkstock.

Printed in the United States of America

WestBow Press rev. date: 9/26/2012

For my mum,
Jackie Crawford

I know she looks on with eager anticipation
of what the Lord will do next.
She always said she loved surprises.
OXO

Contents

Acknowledgements

When given the opportunity to thank those who have helped in this project, I began to reflect upon the different seasons of life I have experienced from the book's inception through to its release. I realized that thanks are due, not only to those who encouraged me through every chapter, but to those who have lovingly mentored me in the ways of the Lord.

Scripture tells us that God delights in using willing vessels to be His hands and feet, and there are many who have been used in this way to impact my life. I cannot express how appreciative I am for the men and women of God who have gone before me, leaving a Godly heritage. Thank you to the trailblazers who dared to speak out for Truth and invested in mentoring the next generation.

I am grateful for the spiritual mothers and fathers the Lord has placed in my life—in particular, Pastors Giulio and Lina Gabeli. They model the true loving heart of the Father, cheering me on to go higher and farther.

Friends are such a great gift from God. Kathy Fraser and Tracy Howard are two who have championed this book from the beginning. Thank you Kathy, for your generous servant heart and your contagious joy. You have always embraced me as part of your family. Tracy, you believe in me and were such an encourager when I needed it most. Thank you for being my head cheerleader!

Thank you to each member of my "book team" who offered valuable feedback, prayers, and Godly wisdom. Shae Cooke's encouragement in the early stages of this book was such a blessing as I began to test my wings as a writer. Thank you Shae for helping me take flight!

I am grateful for the love and support of family. Thank you Lesley for being the big sister that stepped in to help in the early stages of discovery after my diagnosis. Thank you Dad for your encouragement throughout this project, and for your heart of love that wanted to take my place in the treatment chair.

Thank you to my extended family at Westwood Community Church who put their love into action, showing such compassion as I fought the giant of breast cancer.

Lastly, my greatest debt of gratitude is to my beloved Jesus whose love has transformed me. Encountering every facet of the Holy Trinity has, without a doubt, been the greatest experience of my life. Thank you Abba, for choosing me.

Foreword

I n the Arms of My Beloved: A Journey through Breast Cancer is truly an inspirational work from an exceptional person, Sandra Crawford. Her challenge to conquer the giant of breast cancer serves as a reminder that faith, hope, and determination play a key role in overcoming any seemingly insurmountable obstacle in life. Her usage of realism and transparency opens up a doorway for the reader to experience firsthand the emotions, the possible fears, the uncertainty, the disappointments, and questions that arise when a person faces terminal illness. We look into her heart as she recounts the story of her dreams and aspirations as well as the promises she received from the Lord and the subsequent tension of knowing that she could possibly die and not see those promises fulfilled.

Sandra's faith in God is evident as she explains step by step the process of treatment and all the challenges that she faced, seen and unseen. The biblical truths and insights that she shares enrich the readers, whether they are spiritual or secular. She sees her struggle with cancer as being akin to a soldier in boot camp who is given the most difficult assignment of her life—one that will require great courage and bravery.

In this book you will discover precious gems and treasures of truth that will strengthen your faith and stir a hope within you that with God all things are possible. Sandra's blend of humour in the midst of trouble is truly delightful and you may find yourself smiling frequently as you ride an emotional roller coaster of light-hearted moments and times of tears.

I believe that *In the Arms of My Beloved: A Journey through Breast Cancer* is one of the most significant books that deals with the subject of suffering and how to overcome the giant of terminal illness. It is a must-read for professionals and laypersons alike.

Reverend Giulio Gabeli, Senior Pastor,
Westwood Community Church,
Vancouver, Canada

Preface

We travel many roads throughout our lives. Nobody *plans* to go down the wrong path, but we often find ourselves in the midst of situations that could have been avoided if we had made different choices. The journey back onto the right track is often described as one of life's adventures that hopefully enriches our character as well as making us stronger, and wiser. After overcoming the obstacles, we pick up the pieces and forge ahead towards new horizons.

Similarly, few people *expect* to face a life-threatening illness, so when it happens it comes as an unwelcome and inconvenient detour down a road you never thought you would travel. When I was diagnosed with breast cancer, it shook me to the core. It came at a time when I was settling back into a regular routine after spending four years doing short-term missions trips to villages in Mexico and the Philippines, as well as cities in Wales, England, India, Israel, the United States, and Canada. I had developed a deep love for Jesus and had come to know Him as my friend. Old wounds in my soul were healed and peace was finally finding its way into my heart. Returning to the workforce in 2004 I launched into a new career in property management. Less than two years later I was tendering my resignation in favour of developing a strategy for survival. Breast cancer had not been in my plans, so I had no contingency for coping in place.

In the eight years of devotion to Christ, my faith had never been tested to such a degree. I considered myself to be maturing as a Christian, having cleared other hurdles in life, but battling cancer stretched me to a point well beyond my conscious, comfortable limits to a place of total dependence upon God. I understand now why so many people look to a higher power or to God in these times, as cancer is beyond anything we humans can deal with on our own.

I have often heard the words "hope," "courage," and "strength," associated with breast cancer survivors. However the whole part "in between" is rarely mentioned. How does one build and develop these three powerful attributes that enable one to be a survivor? How exactly does one *get* from here to there?

When I became the latest casualty diagnosed with this disease, I felt like I had been washed overboard in the midst of a raging storm. In an attempt to find some answers I started with the easiest resource available: the Internet. Any sense of direction was completely destroyed when my search for "breast cancer" sites returned over 43 million options. How could I possibly sift through this amount of information? Nevertheless I tried, absentmindedly scrolling through various medical journals, testimonies, articles, and statistics. But none of them satisfied my unsettled heart.

In the quietness of my office I pondered what it was exactly that I was looking for. Scientific facts seemed uninteresting, medical reports did not calm me, and testimonies did not move me. I turned off my laptop, closed my eyes and sat in silence until I discovered the true heart of the matter. I wanted to know what *my* future would hold.

Dreams and aspirations were suddenly put on hold as the prospect for tomorrow was grim. As a single woman in my forties who lived alone, I was about to enter a very dangerous battlefield. Having never been married, now more than ever, I longed to have a shoulder that was gentle enough to cry on, yet strong enough to carry my load—someone who completely understood everything that I was feeling and could answer all of my questions. This was so much bigger than any challenge I had ever faced alone and for the first time in my life I questioned if I could succeed.

My search for comfort and truth brought me to the Lord Himself—the source of all hope, all strength, and all courage. The answer was not in a medical journal, but rather in the still small voice of my best friend, Jesus, who promised to walk through the fire with me.

This book is a candid admission of fears and trials in the valley called cancer. It details some life-changing revelations to questions I never knew I had as well as offering some foundational truths about the "whys" of life revealed through the timeless word of God. This is a testimony of God's goodness—His faithfulness and love that have the power to make even the weakest soul an overcomer. I attribute the victory not to my faith in Him, but rather to a surprising confidence He had in me to succeed, proving that we can indeed do all things through Christ.

If you are facing the giant of cancer, perhaps you have many of the same questions and fears and do not know where to start. As you travel through the caverns and gullies of this daunting canyon with me, my hope is that you will grow to love the Lord as you read my account of how, with deep compassion, the Lord reached down and heard my cry. With my head on His chest, I heard His tender heartbeat for me as He lovingly carried me back to the top of the mountain. In complete surrender, I found rest and comfort in the everlasting arms of my beloved Jesus. My hope is that my story will be a single seed of faith that will help you to believe that He will do the same for you.

Introduction

We are all born of God, and have the ability to hear His voice. His word says that as we draw near to God, He will draw near to us. Since becoming a Christian in 1997, I have come to value the truth that God loves us and desires for us to draw near to Him. I think many people would agree that the first time a person actually calls out to God is when he or she is in the midst of trials. The expression, "There are no atheists in foxholes," is a true illustration of our instinct to trust completely in ourselves and our abilities—until the going gets tough!

I believe that the first time we call out to God is quite significant. It is an admission that we need help as well as an initial leap of faith to believe in something or someone who is unseen and who is bigger than us and our problems. We come to a point of desperation and ignore the mocking voices that accuse us of being weak or foolish—such is our desire to know the truth. What began for me as a cry for help developed into a relationship that surpassed anything I could have asked for or imagined. As the Lord unveiled my eyes to see His kingdom, I began to understand I am more than just His daughter—I am enlisted in an army that is establishing His love on earth.

Before being sent to the front lines of any battle, soldiers go through boot camp—vigorous training that prepares them for every type of situation. My first round of basic training was a six month course at a discipleship training school in Kona, Hawaii, with Youth With a Mission (YWAM). As I progressed through the Lord's boot camp, I quickly learned that our spiritual enemy does not like to be pushed aside and I felt him push me back more times than I would like to admit. Whenever he did so I took great joy in knowing that I must be doing something right! As the Lord brought proper alignment to my life I grieved lost relationships and stumbled through the establishment of new ones, learning hard lessons about unconditional love. Instead of walking away from situations, He taught me endurance—to stick around and sort through them. I gradually witnessed my selfish independence fading away in favour of a heart that would not give up on even the most difficult people. Every trial and test was challenging but rewarding as I began to see the fruit of my labour.

Readying myself for graduation, I was anxious to move forward onto greater missions. Short-term trips were fine, however, I felt hindered in the amount I could accomplish in such a small window of time. My heart's desire was to help others find the deep healing that I had found by teaching and mentoring as others had done for me. With all the courses and seminars that I participated in and the studying and prayer that I had been devoted to, I considered myself to be totally abandoned to the ways of the Lord, ready to lay my life down for Christ as He did for me. My next assignment was not at all what I expected and it would prove to be the most difficult trial yet.

My marching orders were handed down: overcome breast cancer. Questions flooded my mind as I braced for the full impact of the news. *I'm just a rookie—would my preparation be sufficient to win a battle of this magnitude? Why would God save me only to hand me over to death? How could a Christian get cancer? Why would He allow this? I thought He loved me.*

God knows what lies beneath our facade, but do we? He knows the outcome, but do we have the faith to believe He will carry us through? I believe the greatest test we can endure is when we face the giant of Death and Destruction, which in my case, came in the form of breast cancer. As we emerge victoriously, we can be confident of all the Lord has done within us and be assured of the ultimate victory over darkness.

Breast cancer certainly had not been on my radar, but the journey changed this warrior forever. I had visited many nations and ministered to thousands, but the most important mission of my life was about to begin in my own home, fighting for my life.

chapter one

Woman of Royal Destiny

Christ in you, the hope of glory.
COLOSSIANS 1:27

"Your biopsy results show a cancerous growth."

This was not what I had hoped to hear from my doctor as I was actively pursuing my God-appointed destiny. But I was sure of one thing: God's promise that He would never leave me. I was about to embark on a journey into unfamiliar territory. Without a road map, I was unsure of the trip and questioned the destination. As I closed my eyes and silently looked to the Lord, I heard, *Christ in me the hope of glory.*

Regardless of the circumstances, I knew I trusted in Him. He is a faithful God whose love is everlasting. As I ventured into the fire, the Lord went with me and at every corner, in every detail, He was there. He became more than the sustainer of life and the lifter of my head; He became my confidant and friend and proved beyond any doubt that He loves me more than anyone ever could. I knew with certainty that He would work all these things together for good.

In the beginning...
On March 22, 2006, I discovered a lump in my right breast. I was not panicked as my family had no history of breast cancer, and it

never occurred to me that I might have breast cancer. A fairly healthy person, I rarely needed the services of a doctor. Still, the discovery disturbed me and so I called my family physician who suggested that it was just a cyst—not to worry. However, to be safe, she arranged for a mammogram. During the next two weeks I tried not to think about it too much, however I found myself checking the lump every ten minutes or so to see if it was still there.

The day finally arrived for the mammogram—my first, so the entire procedure was new to me. The x-ray was done at a small hospital in Vancouver that definitely turned out to be the Lord's choice, one of many indications of His watchful eye upon me. I checked in at the registration desk and took a seat in the large lobby area. The fingerprints of the Lord were everywhere, in scripture and biblical pictures on every wall of the waiting room, a sign of His closeness that gave me great peace.

They called me into an area designated for patients only and then directed me to the changing room in preparation for the exam. Unlike the lobby waiting room that was bright and comfortable, I waited on a hard plastic chair in a cold, dimly lit hallway. The standard-issue hospital gown came fresh out of the warming oven, which was a great comfort in the ominous corridor. Such a small, insignificant act helped immeasurably amidst the tension that was beginning to sneak in. It felt like a warm hug, settling any fears and restlessness. This was the beginning of many medical visits where I would brusquely be directed to strip down to my waist and put on a gown. While waiting my turn, I witnessed many people being shuffled swiftly around by orderlies from one room to another. I sensed an unspoken connection between us; as patients, we were all grasping at any opportunity to be distracted. The moving gurneys were close to my eye level, so my instinct was to make eye contact with each person and offer a smile as they rolled past. This simple gesture seemed to transcend words, offering a brief moment of life and light to their day. Helping others has always been a coping mechanism for me to alleviate tension, as it takes my attention off myself and focuses it on the needs of others. It invariably turned a long, lonely wait into an opportunity for joy and blessing.

After the humiliating experience of having my breasts flattened on a cold, metal surface and then photographed for what they called a mammogram, I was sent back into the hallway to wait again. I felt a bit troubled as they decided to move up the date of my ultrasound to that very same day. I know people often criticize the healthcare system, but in my case those responsible certainly addressed my situation immediately. (And I am sure God had something to do with it too!) On the move again, I was shuffled off into a new examination room for a more thorough inspection of the lump. With all the doctors, nurses, and interns I faced in nine months of treatment, I never got used to being asked to disrobe before strangers. I tried to remind myself that I was just another body to them, which did not always help me in my ongoing struggle of self-worth. In fact, it slowly brought me shame as I tried to mentally disconnect from what was going on.

The room was fairly dark, with only enough light to read the ultrasound monitor. I was positioned on the bed in such a way that I could see the screen. As I was not really sure what I was looking at, I would shift my glance from the monitor over to the technician, looking for answers in his response. Their medical training must teach them how to remain unaffected by every new discovery of a cancerous tumour, as his facial expressions did not tell me a thing.

He took a couple of snapshots and then called in a doctor for an assessment. Although they remained unemotional, I felt the tension of their discovery. When they were done, I asked for a copy of the picture for my records. The technician seemed a bit surprised by my request but graciously went down the hall to copy it for me. A shock of reality hit me hard. I had always imagined my first ultrasound photo to be of a child in my womb, not a lump in my breast. An appointment was scheduled the following week for a biopsy of the lump, a delay that suited me just fine, as I already felt the burden of too much information to process.

Two days later, I spoke at our church's ladies group, the Women of Royal Destiny. I have always loved this name since it reflects the Lord's great delight in our realization of who we are in Him. As daughters of the King (Jesus), we have an appointed inheritance and a destiny as royalty in His kingdom. I felt honoured to share some testimonies of my life and bring an encouraging word for those in attendance. I decided not to divulge my latest discovery to anyone and instead focused on the greatness of God and the power of His might.

I had prayed much, waiting on the Lord for several days to be sure of the topic He wanted me to speak about that evening. As it turned out, I had an opportunity to test the very testimony I uttered as I made mention of the shipwreck in the book of Acts. In this story, the apostle Paul had been imprisoned in Caesarea and was being transferred by ship to Rome. Along the way, they encountered tempestuous seas and gale-force winds that threatened the lives of all those onboard. His was the voice of assurance when panic began to spread through the ranks. In the midst of the raging storm, Paul's faith and confidence proved unshakable.

> But now I urge you to keep up your courage, because not one of you will be lost; only the ship will be destroyed (Acts 27:22).

The ship started to break up on the rocks and, clinging to planks and boards, "Everyone reached land in safety" (Acts 27:44).

The soldiers had it in their mind to kill the prisoners, yet their lives were spared by the hand of God (vv. 42–43). The Lord raised up a godly man, a prisoner named Paul, to speak the truth and lead the entire group to safety while strengthening and encouraging them. The enemy (Satan) wanted to *kill* Paul, but the Lord spared his life. I also talked about the spiritual battle we, as believers, are engaged in and the Lord's boot camp of preparation.

> For we wrestle not against flesh and blood, but against principalities, against powers, against the rulers of the darkness of this age, against spiritual hosts of wickedness in heavenly places (Ephesians 6:12 NKJV®).

Regardless of what we believe, a constant war is being fought between light and darkness, good and evil, and God and Satan, and you and I are in the midst of it. We may not choose to participate, but the war goes on and usually involves us as our adversary, Satan, tries to secure dominion over the earth.

For years I had unknowingly allowed the enemy to rule my life, luring me with false promises of happiness. As I had been brought up with a strong work ethic, my dedication and hard work positioned me for fast promotions, affording me the opportunity to travel abroad and secure a healthy bank account. I realized that although we can feel a measure of liberty in making our own decisions, the goals we set often involve material wealth or worldly love. After recognizing that the lusts of this world are fleeting, I began to engage in a battle for true liberty that can only be found in God.

Shortly after embarking on my new life as a Christian, I began to read the "draftee's survival guide," more commonly known as the Bible. I uncovered many truths about what it means to be part of God's kingdom and the rules of engagement when fighting off the enemy. It blew my stereotypical idea of the "quiet Christian" right out of the water.

Many years ago, I bought into the commonly held perception that for the most part, Christians were well-mannered, well-meaning people who went to church on Sunday, sat in a pew, sang a few songs, listened to a sermon, and every now and then told others that they needed Jesus. They did their best to be kind, so much so that in their desire to be loving and turn the other cheek, they often allowed others to walk all over them.

Joining the dots between what I knew to be the quiet, passive Christian and those who are bold, radical lovers of God is a process that still continues for me. The more I studied who God is, the more I understood the authority He gives us and the mandate He has decreed for the kingdom of God to be established on the earth. This can only be accomplished by intimately knowing the character of God and possessing these same qualities. As we surrender with complete trust to the Lord's ways, we undergo a transformation that gives us a voice to speak with boldness and creates in us a confidence to succeed.

After launching into this new lifestyle of a total commitment to Jesus, I began to realize that many never understand, or walk in, the full power of God that is available to us. The Lord does not want us to be passive or naïve as the enemy schemes against us, but rather to grasp hold of the truth and understand that God's power resides within us.

> I have given you authority to trample on snakes and scorpions and to overcome all the power of the enemy; nothing will harm you (Luke 10:19).

When discovering the snares that so easily entangled me, I began to see how they even had the power to change my personality, slowly leading into the darkness of depression. An unwillingness to forgive had led to bitterness and resentment, and years of rejection had turned a confident leader into a sad, withdrawn soul. When I learned of the authority that I have in prayer to cast down the fortresses of lies the enemy had built in my mind, I began to send him packing! The life of a Christian is not just about a relationship with the Lord—it is an opportunity to take back what belongs to us. For me, it was to discover the truth of who God created me to be.

The word of God says that the thief, Satan, comes to "steal, kill, and destroy" (John 10:10). Now that I am aware of a very real adversary, I am on high alert and ready to stand against his assaults. I believe the Lord is raising up men and women of valour who will grab hold of these truths and plunder the enemy's camp, living a life of victory.

That evening, I shared a photo of an old World War II poster from Britain appealing to women to join the labour force while the men were fighting on the front lines. Women took jobs in factories, farms, shipyards, and munitions depots, filling many positions previously held by men. They also served in the armed forces and proved to be a great strength to the war effort.

The dictionary defines courage as:
> readiness to face and capacity to endure danger,
> inherent freedom from fear or from its disturbing
> effects, (*have the ~ of one's convictions,* be ready to
> declare or act upon them; venture boldly).

And valour is defined as:
> courage, especially in battle.

Drawing on my own experiences, I explained how the Lord called me and taught me to use the weapons He had placed in my hands. By His grace, there are many rounds of boot camp and just as many seasons for promotion. As I spoke, I knew that my opportunity for promotion was upon me.

I returned home that evening still stirring from the residual effects of ministering for the Lord. My spirit was dancing too much for me to sleep and so I sat in my favourite chair in front of the fireplace, spending time with Jesus. I asked Him the question that I had not had the courage to ask until this moment.

Is it cancer?

I do not always trust myself to hear a straight "yes" or "no" from God, as my own emotions and desires can get in the way of hearing clearly. I do, however, trust the word of God. As I waited in silence, I suddenly heard *1 Peter 4:1*. It is not often that I hear scripture references so clearly, but this night it seemed to drop into my spirit. We all have the ability to hear from God, and I believe there is an exceptional favour and grace that rests upon us in troublesome times to hear His Spirit directing us. Not knowing that particular scripture from memory, I anxiously opened my Bible and flipped to it.

> Therefore, since Christ suffered in his body, arm
> yourselves also with the same attitude, because he
> who has suffered in his body is done with sin.

I knew I had heard from heaven—this was not me, but the Lord answering my question. Although it was not what I wanted to hear, a quiet resolve took root within me as I knew His closeness. In that moment, my best friend quieted my soul with His love. Jesus' peace overwhelmed me as I braced myself to "suffer in my body" for reasons that only God Himself understood.

The date for my first biopsy arrived. Having previously visited the hospital for tests, the anxieties and fears of the initial visit were somewhat abated. Sitting in the same spot in the waiting room, I picked up a Reader's Digest™, hoping to find some comic relief in the short stories columns. When they called my name I walked down the hall, turned left at the changing room, grabbed a smock fresh from the oven, stripped down to the waist and waited again. After a few moments, they ushered me into the room where they had previously performed the ultrasound, although this time they were armed with a huge weapon they referred to as a needle.

I can do this. I can do this.

Generally, I was the person who tried to put the *doctors* at ease, as I often felt the awkwardness of the situation. Humour had a way of successfully breaking the ice before a stranger engaged in touching a very private part of me, so in an effort to lighten the atmosphere, I engaged in light banter with the two ultrasound specialists.

For this exam I again positioned myself on my back, right arm bent, with my hand beneath my head and my breast exposed to the attending technician. He inserted the needle into the tumour to retrieve what is referred to as a "core sample." (I hoped they would find gold, but my refining was not yet complete!) It sounded like a staple gun as they gingerly harvested their samples. Fortunately he did not need to use the larger needle as just the *sound* of it was too daunting for me. The results would take a week—another opportunity to wait. I certainly found myself learning patience on this slow road to discovery.

Nine days later I received the dreaded phone call from my doctor's office requesting that I come in to meet with her. Thankfully she made time for me that same day so that I did not have to try to sleep on it for one more night. As I sat across from her she slowly opened the manila file folder and informed me that they had found cancerous cells in the tumour. The ensuing conversation seemed very businesslike as we discussed timelines and options.

I calmly asked a couple of questions, not really knowing where to start. I remember hearing "surgery and chemotherapy," followed by "radiation." I could expect to be involved in treatment until the end of the year or perhaps into January. We set up two appointments, one to meet with the surgeon and a second for a more extensive biopsy to obtain information about the type of cancer I had. As I left her office and drove home, the thoughts of the daunting task that lay ahead filled my mind: I needed to break the news to my family. Jesus had prepared me, but I was not sure how my family would react.

I called home and Mum answered the phone. My parents had been on high alert for the past few weeks, anxiously following the process of my medical visits. Dad picked up the extension phone so they could both hear the news together. There is no easy way for a daughter to announce to her parents that she has cancer, so I simply took a breath and spoke the truth as gently as I knew how. Mum has always been the talkative one and was quick to offer comfort, but I found myself drawn more to Dad's silence and my eyes welled up as I heard him stifle back his own tears. Dad is a very proud man with a gentle spirit, and I know him well enough to say that he felt helpless at that moment—there was nothing he could do for the daughter he loved. As he composed himself, he uttered the words that could only have come from the very heart of Jesus. With sincerity he said,

"If I could take your place, I would."

Knowing my dad, I believed him.

A few days later I returned to the hospital for the second biopsy, feeling even more confident in knowing the routine. The appointment was late afternoon so I decided to go straight from work. It was good to be working as it kept my mind from wandering down too many "what if" paths. Never losing sight of the spiritual battle at hand, I remained diligent about saying my prayers of coverage before entering the hospital. I would put on the armour of God (dressed for battle), cleanse every room (and everything in it) by the blood of Jesus, and affirm that the presence of the Lord was with me.[1]

Soon I was back on the table in what was becoming a familiar room: lights dimmed and ultrasound machine ready to go. This time a second technician was present as an assistant. Still not over my embarrassment of disrobing in front of strangers, I again tried to make light of it. As they went to work, the assistant picked up on my efforts and proceeded to make a few humorous remarks, which became inappropriate in nature. Initially I did not challenge where he was going with his comments, but they soon made me feel uncomfortable. The technician attempted to take the core sample but soon ran into difficulty as the larger needle was not able to penetrate the cancerous part of the tumour—it seemed to be as hard as a rock. The assistant, who was standing on the left side of the bed, then leaned directly over me, and pressed on my chest as the technician on my right seemed to put all of his weight over the needle to penetrate the tumour. They clearly struggled to get the needle in place and in their distress joked about the situation.

I felt violated but too embarrassed to speak and even began to question who the assistant was as he was dressed in regular street clothes rather than a hospital coat. After they finally succeeded in obtaining a sample, I felt a great sense of relief as they left the room. Quickly wiping the messy ultrasound gel off my chest, I threw on my clothes and headed for the door, holding back the tears until I reached the safety of my car.

Shaking uncontrollably, the tears began to flow, releasing some of the stress and fear I had just experienced. I cried out to the Lord and He met me as I sat alone in my car—the comfort of the Holy Spirit embracing me as I reassessed what had just occurred. I am a slow, methodical thinker so it took me time to process the experience and see how many things were so wrong about it. However, any

---

[1] See the Declarations of Truth in Appendix A for more information on prayers of coverage and other kinds of prayer.

opportunity to speak up had passed, so I could only deal with the fallout. A spirit of fear and trauma had assaulted me, and so I prayed through the situation until it lifted, remembering to forgive the technician and his assistant for their behaviour, and myself for not speaking up. Then, using the authority that Christ gave me, I rebuked fear and trauma, sending them to the place of their demise—the foot of the cross. I felt the relief come but still remained weary from the intense battle and its after-effects.

Turning the key in the ignition, I took a deep breath and began the long drive home. I was pleased to have this horrible experience behind me and thankful to have rush hour traffic to take my mind off the day. Staring at the taillights of the car ahead of me I thought, *How could this possibly be the road for a Woman of Royal Destiny?*

chapter two

Choices

No eye has seen, no ear has heard, no mind has
conceived what God has prepared for those who love
him, but God has revealed it to us by his Spirit.
1 CORINTHIANS 2:9-10

This was one of the first promises the Lord placed in my heart in the early years of becoming a Christian. It filled me with such hope and expectation for what was yet to come, for He is a good God who loves me. How exciting it will be, I thought, to see His plans and purposes unfold in my life!

I have learned that the Lord does nothing by chance, but performs all things in love, with exceptional skill and lasting effects. As I confessed my desire to follow Him with complete abandonment, He began a profound work of healing my broken heart from years of suppressed hurts and deep wounds. As the Lord brought truth to my innermost being, the ways of the world fell away, thereby revealing a beautiful vessel, fit to carry His glory and His love. Over the past ten years I have been high on the mountaintops receiving His love and joy, and deep in the valleys as my sins and unhealthy thought patterns were painfully stripped away. Through this necessary process known as sanctification, I have experienced a transformation that has enriched my life beyond anything I have ever experienced. Only as old wounds are healed do we find a peace that is beyond our understanding and the ability to touch others with this powerful life-changing love. Just as the refiner thrusts the metal into the fire to burn away the dross, so the Lord works out all our imperfections by turning up the heat. (I have been in and out of the refiner's fire so often I could collect air miles!)

When I worked as a software trainer, I had the privilege of traveling extensively, which planted an insatiable desire in me to see more of the world. With every new culture I became immersed in, I developed a deep love for the diversity of God's people—His many tribes and nations. As I have a heart to help and teach, I have always believed that He would use me to help make disciples of all nations—the Great Commission that is spoken of in Matthew 28.

However, after having been a Christian for more than five years, I often struggled with discouragement as I tried to determine where I *belonged* in His kingdom. I felt like the prodigal who had returned home only to find that the party was over after a few short months. My zeal for the Lord offended many and I came to realize that many churchgoers pray for the return of the prodigals, but do not want to give them a voice. Instead of finding a place of healing, I discovered that some of the deepest wounding came at the hands of God's people. This confused me and caused me to withdraw.

I have come to understand that those with a sincere heart of compassion will take the time to disciple and teach the zealous the ways of the Lord. Those spiritual mothers and fathers possess a true heart of love and want to see God's children advance and be released into the fullness of their destiny. The commitment and total abandonment of a prodigal towards her heavenly Father is precious in the eyes of the Lord. It is this truth that has propelled me onwards in my desire to serve the God of Love and has kept my eyes focused on Him alone rather than putting my hope in groups of people. This valuable lesson was an integral part of the foundation the Lord laid within me.

Although I experienced the supernatural hand of God as I ventured onto the mission field, I always felt that there was something more—that I was just scratching the surface. Deep within me remained a question of where and how the Lord would use me. The seasons came and went as I continued to learn about the many facets of the Lord and ventured out on many short-term mission trips, helping in whatever capacity I could. I watched others carrying on with their lives, each getting married, having children, and finding joy and purpose. Still, I strongly sensed that I was missing the boat—I was not even sure if I had found the water!

Holding on to the promises of God became difficult as one year drifted into another with little change in my compass heading. At forty-four, I always thought I would be married and have a family of my own, or at the very least, know what I was going to be when I grew up! In an attempt to get over my disappointment of not being a mum, I clung to the promise that the Lord had something in store for me: great plans, a hope, and a future. My strength waned at times, yet my heart whispered, *Just a little longer. Your time is coming. Keep believing.* However, sometimes I felt as if I was clinging to the edge of a cliff and my fingers were tiring. *It would be so easy to just let go.*

Receiving the diagnosis of breast cancer shook me out of my complacency and caused me to ask many questions of *myself,* including whether or not I was still prepared to hold on.

The Lord always gives us a choice and that day I was surprised to be asked,

Will you choose life or death?

Did I want to live, or give into death? This might seem like a ridiculous question. The obvious answer is to choose life. The very fact that I would entertain the idea of allowing death to overtake me revealed a lifetime of disappointments that could no longer remain hidden.

Wouldn't it be lovely to drift off into eternity in heaven with my beloved Jesus? Through every step of the refining fire, I am certain of my love for Him as I continue to draw closer to my beloved. But, the truth is, I do not need to live out my days on earth just to know His love. What is the plan for my life? Have I missed the boat of blessing, or will I believe it is still headed my way?

It is one thing to live a life of obedience to the Lord, but a different level of commitment is achieved by *owning* His vision for us. The Lord knows I would go anywhere, give anything, and do whatever He asked of me. The only problem was that I had not yet discovered my calling. I had explored many avenues, giving my all to every new project or mission, yet each new challenge seemed to be a distraction to my real purpose—not quite hitting the mark.

I have come to believe that many of God's children fall into this category of waiting and wondering. My complete trust in the Lord had caused me to take a back seat in the responsibility of navigating my future so I had become complacent in the season of waiting. As time ticked away I began to lose zeal, and unbelief started sneaking in unnoticed. My heart questioned if I would ever be ready, or if I had missed my opportunity since I was a late bloomer, not finding Him until I was thirty-five years old.

Knowing these questions were milling around in my mind, I believe the Lord took this opportunity to share a deeper revelation of *His* heart behind the calling on my life. But first, He needed me to confess my willingness to live. Out of His great love for me, He began to speak to me as His friend.

I know the Lord is calling an army of saints who love Him, but would I carry on with a cheerful heart on the front lines? Could my zeal be resurrected? By His grace He presented me with two options. There was seriousness in the moment, as I knew I stood at a crossroad of my destiny. After I made a move, there would be no turning back, but regardless of what I decided I knew He would still love me.

Truth was staring me squarely in the face as I arrived at this junction of decision. The choices were clear:

Easy Street: *HEAVEN* or Rocky Road: *EARTH*

I believe heaven to be a place of joy—no more tears or sorrows; a place free of struggles and where love abounds along with light and life. There is no striving, no disappointments, no loneliness, no challenges, no rejection, no financial hardships, and no death. To choose the alternative, to stay and live out my days on earth, required a level of courage and strength that I was not sure I could ever attain. I seemed too easily discouraged and disappointed throughout my life. I had fought a good fight, but was weary, and the enemy knew it. Could I ever see myself achieving all that I hoped for—all the promises of God that had been spoken over my life? Did I have faith to believe them as truth? I trusted in the Lord, but wavered in the confidence I had in myself to fulfill all that He asked of me.

The apostle Paul said,

> For me, to live is Christ and to die is gain
> (Philippians 1:21).

The second half of this statement did not scare me, as I had no fear of dying. I believed I would willingly lay down my life for another if the Lord asked me to, or if infirmity overtook me. I welcomed the opportunity to see my Jesus!

"To live is Christ." Hmm—a very weighty statement that answers the age old question, "What is the meaning of life?" A great sacrifice before the Lord would be to offer my *whole* life up to Him for His purposes. I could no longer compromise the amount I chose to surrender to the Lord—it was all or nothing. My life would no longer be lived on my terms; so every last bit of my selfish desires would have to be surrendered as an act of my complete trust in Him.

In order to live out my days on earth I could no longer drift aimlessly, hoping to make a difference to anyone who came near my boat. I needed to find my rudder and set a clear course; to live with a purpose and passion that would bring life and liberty to lost, dying souls.

To face the daily struggles that come with living in a fallen world, I needed to be sure of my identity *in Him*. I had reached a level of sanctification that would only be enough to get by, so the Lord was asking me to make a choice. If I went back in the furnace, the heat was going to be turned up to a level that would require complete trust and faith in Him.

> And from the days of John the Baptist until now the
> kingdom of heaven suffers violence, and the violent
> take it by force (Matthew 11:12 NKJV®).

To be a soldier of the Lord requires spiritual courage, valour, perseverance, and strength. I had wrestled with the enemy in the past and won, but I had also felt his sting.

This end time battlefield is like no other generation before us. In my mind's eye a vision unfolded . . . *Troops were assembling. I felt a stirring in my spirit of fear mixed with anxiety. Multitudes of soldiers, armour and weapons swept across the expanse of the plain. Horses were restless, sensing the magnitude of what was just ahead. The chatter faded* . . . I struggled to make sense of my thoughts and the vision that seemed so close.

The battle belongs to the Lord, but could He use my hands and feet? I knew in my mind the truth of the Lord's triumph, but I questioned if I had the courage to strike when and how the Lord commanded. Could He make a violent warrior in the spirit out of a gentle soul? I needed to lay hold of this victory in my heart before advancing.

The word of God is our handbook, so I went back to a very simple promise He gave me six years ago.

> The One who calls you is faithful and He will do it
> (1 Thessalonians 5:24).

My thoughts wandered to the scene in the garden of Gethsemane on the eve of Christ's crucifixion.

> Then he [Jesus] said to them, "My soul is overwhelmed
> with sorrow to the point of death. Stay here and keep
> watch with me" (Matthew 26:38).

As the apostle Paul states in 2 Corinthians 5:14, it is *Christ's* love that compels us.

Meditating on these truths, I considered Jesus in the garden. Even the Son of God struggled with the battle before Him. I concluded that the Father had to deposit within Him a level of love that propelled Him forth to complete the task ahead. It was the *agape* love of our heavenly Father that carried Jesus to the cross and gave Him strength to endure until it was finished; for it is *this* kind of perfect love that casts out all fear (1 John 4:18).

The only way I could continue with my commission was with this same kind of love that was not from this realm, but from the throne of heaven—a love that conquers all. This kind of weapon cannot be found in the enemy's camp, as he is incapable of love. Yes, this was our secret weapon of war: LOVE!

As I made my petition before heaven for this "Gethsemane love," I realized that it is our key to victory. This is the foundation upon which our character is built—evidence of God's heart taking shape within us. As our level of intimacy with Him develops, we walk in more authority. *This* is the type of army He is training. His warriors will take the kingdom by force; not by violent *assaults,* but by violent *love. This* is the love that will compel me. This all encompassing, unconditional perfect love is the love that will conquer all.

As Moses said to the Lord,

> If your Presence does not go with us, do not send us
> up from here (Exodus 33:15).

Before the Lord and His heavenly host of angels, I declared my choice to run the race assigned to me—the Narrow, Rocky Road. Though it would be wrought with unknown curves, I would be accompanied by the King and assured of victory.

Walking back into the fire

Within a week I was scheduled to meet with the surgeon. The pathology report from the second biopsy was in and I needed to make some decisions. Upon hearing the news of my breast cancer, my sister Lesley volunteered to be my point person—someone to accompany me to all medical appointments. She is often moved by the plight of others, so naturally wanted to do something to help. I am independent by nature but quickly accepted her offer, as clearly two heads would be better than one. Lesley is four years my senior and my only sibling. We are compatible even though we have different interests and while we do not spend much time together, we easily chat about life when we do connect.

Unsure of how rush hour might delay our trip into the city, we arrived for my appointment over an hour early. After parking the car, we decided to wait in the coffee shop next door—the first of many cups of coffee we would have as we wished the time away. Wondering what the next few hours would hold we pondered every scenario, speculating answers the experts might offer. Lesley and I had the same level of knowledge on the subject, which did not amount to much. Most of it consisted of facts and statistics we had gleaned from the Internet over the past couple of weeks. Lesley's previous experiences with the healthcare system had not left her with much confidence, as she had lost her husband shortly after routine surgery. Now she faced similar fears as she sat across the table wondering about the fate of her sister. We found common ground with giants of the same name.

The surgeon was highly respected in her field, which brought some level of comfort to us. Our visit started off on an awkward foot due to some confusion in the front office. When we arrived, we found the outer door of the office locked, as the assistant was late into work. Our appointment time came and went as we stood out in the hallway, looking longingly through the small glass window beside the door. We finally saw someone near reception and so we knocked on the door, attempting to get her attention. The doctor, unaware that her assistant had not yet arrived, begrudgingly let us in, seemingly annoyed that we were "late." Her brusque demeanour did little to settle my nerves as we followed her into the examination room. She did not spend much time looking over the pathology report but proceeded right to her examination and recommendations.

The cancer was classified as a high-grade, triple negative, invasive type of cancer that was quickly spreading, so the priority was to remove the tumour as soon as possible. The doctor presented us with two choices: a lumpectomy (removal of the tumour), or a total mastectomy (removal of the entire breast). We discussed the pros and cons quickly and efficiently and decided to do a lumpectomy. The surgeon then signed a requisition for blood work and a second order for a chest x-ray. After settling on a surgery date and receiving a comprehensive folder of additional information, we were out the door. There was little time to think about what we were hearing with a barrage of information, delivered faster than my mind could process. Doctors must deal with so many patients in a day that they can easily become disconnected from compassion and suppress any outward display of emotion. Perhaps that is how they cope with the staggering number of new cancer victims that walk into their offices each week.

On the receiving end, it is easy to become overwhelmed by all the terminology and facts being presented in such a short period of time. While the surgeon was discussing the options, I found it difficult to keep up and was grateful to have Lesley with me to catch anything I might have missed. We were a great team: she would write, and I would run interference with my copious questions. Any hesitation in the conversation would certainly mean a conclusion to our meeting, so we grappled for our questions, anxiously wanting to cover all the bases before leaving. When a pause found its way into the flood of questions, we did a coach-to-player glance, silently asking, "Did we forget anything?" We felt confident that we had asked all the right questions on a subject we knew virtually nothing about.

Armed with our books, pamphlets, forms, requisitions, and notepads, we headed out the door with our first assignment: a blood test, one floor up. It was a relief just to have left the tornado of her office. With our minds buzzing, we stood at the elevator in silence. We felt like country bumpkins who had just been dropped off in downtown New York with roadmaps and brochures, not knowing where to start.

Anxious to begin the phone campaign to deliver the news, Lesley stepped outside to make calls while I sorted through the variety of coloured papers for the lab requisition. After the blood test, I ventured down two floors for the chest x-ray—or was it up one floor? My natural talent for organization and multi-tasking failed miserably as I struggled to keep the slips of paper together and not leave them as a trail behind me. My enormous list of "to dos" seemed to bypass my conscious mind, reverting to the survival mode of autopilot.

For the second time that day I was disrobing to be examined. As I sat in the waiting room I tried to collect my thoughts, allowing everything to sink in. To pick up a magazine for casual reading would have overloaded my brain, so I found a place on the floor to stare at until I heard my name called.

After searching two floors Lesley finally found me: another office in another waiting room, patiently waiting for word that I was released. They confirmed my x-ray film was good, and so I was permitted to dress and leave. I felt emotionally drained by the activities of the last couple of hours so my first few steps out onto the busy Vancouver sidewalk were a welcome relief. The warm sun and fresh air seemed to breathe new life into me.

As we walked towards the car, I caught a glimpse of a familiar face coming towards us, and quickly searched my memory for her name. I hesitated to greet her, still feeling fragile, yet I sensed that this was a divine appointment. Generally, these "God moments" give me an opportunity to bless someone with a prayer or word of encouragement, but today I was on the receiving end.

I knew her as a woman of prayer and felt the safety to reach out to her that afternoon. We were just acquaintances but we had an immediate connection with our hearts for the Lord. I barely got out the words to explain my diagnosis and she embraced me with the arms of Jesus. My tears flowed as Lynne prayed such a beautiful prayer of comfort. The faithfulness of the Lord should not surprise me, but I confess He often shows up when I am not expecting Him. After we parted, I felt as though I had just stood beneath a "cleansing waterfall" and realized that Lynne had lived up to the meaning of her name, which means just that. I recalled so many sidewalk prayers I had offered people over the years, wondering if they had ever made any difference. That particular day I understood how a kind word in season can bring great comfort and peace to a fearful and weary soul.

The next morning I drove into work and busied myself with client calls and the growing stack of work on my desk. Again I found myself on autopilot as I tried to keep my thoughts from wandering. Focusing on my computer monitor, I reached to answer the phone and heard my sister's voice invading my absent minded routine to ask,

"How are you today?"

It was as though a rock had just shattered the protective glass that had surrounded me for the past twenty-four hours. The floodgates opened as I burst into tears, sobbing uncontrollably. Shock had made its way in unnoticed and I ceased functioning, becoming disconnected and confused. Trivial customer complaints seemed insignificant in light of the death sentence I felt that I had just been handed.

It was Thursday, so I excused myself from work for the next two days in order to gain some composure and perspective over the weekend. My employer called me that evening, suggesting that I look into medical benefits offered by the government since I did not have an extended medical plan. I had not even begun to think about the monetary aspect of being sick, but felt the responsibility to have an answer for her by Monday since I had taken time off to sort things out. After tracking down the appropriate government agency, successfully selecting all the correct phone options, and listening to a lot of elevator music, I finally reached a live person who was able to answer all my questions. I learned that the province would cover me for fifteen weeks at 50 percent of my current wage. My foggy brain was pleased to have found an answer while the rest of my body craved sleep due to fatigue.

The next morning my employer called me again, inviting me for lunch. Still feeling weary, I sat across the table, unable to give definitive answers to all her questions about how this would impact my ability to work or if I was taking a leave of absence. Knowing that they are trying to run a business I felt obliged to give them the whole picture, but was unable to see it myself. I simply did not have all the answers and was not sure my mind was clear enough to make an informed decision. However, by the end of our conversation I had agreed to leave the company in two weeks—the day before surgery. They were free to hire a replacement, not having to depend upon the uncertainty of my commitment for the next nine months. Everything was moving so fast. I barely had enough time to check in with the Lord on what His will was for me in the midst of all the decisions I suddenly had to make. I just had to trust that He was behind the wheel of this fast-moving car, plotting the course and destination, and I was simply a passenger, buckled in and hoping to remain in an upright position until the next turn.

Knowing the power of praise, I found the strength to sing to the Lord for nearly an hour that evening, but the comfort of His presence eluded me well into the night. *Where are you Lord?* I longed to feel His closeness; this was not a time for more testing. When I awoke on Saturday morning, something had lifted and the air was clear again. The truth of His word came to me.

We live by faith, not by sight (2 Corinthians 5:7).

I will never leave you nor forsake you (Joshua 1:5).

He was teaching me not to depend on my feelings. I must *know* He is near because His word says so. The Lord never misses an opportunity to teach us His ways!

I asked the Lord for wisdom and understanding about the whirlwind of changes. As I waited upon Him, He picked me up, dusted me off, and spoke to my heart.

It had to happen this way.

Jesus came as our redeemer. He was a king deserving royal treatment and yet was born in a stable. He was scorned, beaten, bruised, and mocked on the road to the cross. He accomplished all He was sent to do, yet He endured great hardship and abuse. We might wonder why Jesus had to walk such a harsh road, but it had to happen that way, just as it had been foretold by the prophets. The most gruelling trials in His life occurred on the days leading up to His greatest triumph.

As I pondered this truth I began to see that I was on the verge of discovering my own destiny. This was not just a bump in the road; it was my final exam before my promotion. His hand had released me from my job, allowing me to focus completely on the task at hand: winning this battle for my life.

chapter three

Surgery

I will repay you for the years the locusts have eaten.
JOEL 2:25

The day of my surgery finally arrived, May 19. Whenever I would go to the mission field or just on holiday, Dad would be my airport chauffeur. This has evolved into an area of ministry that he fully embraces. Today he was driving me again, but this time our destination was the hospital. Mum and Lesley also came along to show their support, which reminded me of the blessings of family.

We arrived at the small hospital by 6:30 a.m. and were the first at the front door—so early that nobody was there to let us in. When the doors finally opened, we made our way to the waiting room while the clerks at the reception desk got themselves organized for the day. Other patients started to stream in and the chairs quickly filled to capacity. Although the setting was comfortable, each of us was keenly aware of why we were there: you or someone you were with was having surgery. I had prayed intermittently that morning from the time I stepped into the shower until my arrival at the hospital. In tense times like these I call out to the Lord, asking Him to draw near to me. His calming presence is a great comfort, particularly when I do not know what I am facing and He does.

As I looked around the waiting room assessing the other surgery candidates, I was surprised to realize that I was sitting directly across from three large paintings on the wall that confirmed the closeness of my beloved Jesus. In the centre picture, Jesus was looking right at "me" with his arms extended, with the same love and compassion as the Father welcoming home His prodigal daughter. The picture to the right depicted Him standing amongst all kinds of professionals: doctors, nurses, and business workers. The illustration to the left spoke directly to my heart. It was a scene from an operating room. Amid the bright lights, a surgery was in full swing. Nurses in their hospital scrubs were busily attending to the procedure while a figure dressed in white was leaning over the shoulder of the surgeon, directing his every move. Instantly, the joy of the Lord overwhelmed me and I laughed out loud at this special delivery message sent directly to me. I felt Him winking at me as if to say, *Do not worry, I have got every detail covered.*

"Sandra Crawford." It was my turn. Off I went to meet with the surgeon so she could take her big black marker and draw the incision line on my chest where the tumour was to be removed. Then they shuffled me down to a bed at the end of the ward where I was to wait my turn before entering the operating room. They handed me the standard issue surgical wardrobe: a powder-blue robe that is not at *all* discrete about tying in the back, and lovely warm booties that stretched up to my knees. The nurses fussed to get answers to what seemed like endless questions, and then the good-byes came. My family gathered around my bed to wish me a temporary farewell, knowing that I was safely in the care of the Great Physician Himself, Jesus. It was comforting to know that they too, trusted in the Lord enough to place me in His hands.

I was blessed in so many ways to be the first patient into the operating room that day. I am always aware of the spiritual residue that can be left behind by people, so wherever I find myself, whether in a hotel room or airplane seat, I speak a cleansing prayer over everything. This was an early lesson I learned about preparing for battle in the Lord's army.[2] In Matthew 12:43, Jesus tells us, "When an evil spirit comes out of a man, it goes through arid places seeking rest and does not find it." I believe that many of these types of spirits manifest themselves in sickness and infirmity, so one of my first prayers that morning was to ask the Lord to bless and cleanse the operating room.

After being wheeled down the hallway to "holding area one," I recognized some of the faces I had seen on the other side of the double doors. Another curtain was drawn and it was time to wait again. I could hear lots of activity, then *whoosh!* went the curtain and I was on the move again, this time to my final destination: the operating room with its trillion-watt lights. The peace that I experienced there pleasantly surprised me. The smell of the disinfectant seemed to confirm that Jesus had gone ahead of me and prepared the room. (Although, this was not *really* what I had in mind when He said He would go ahead to prepare a place for me!) Being the first patient of the day also meant that I would have more time to recover before they sent me home the next afternoon—another provision from the Lord.

The operating room nurses lifted me from the gurney and set me onto the hard, narrow, operating table, where they strapped my legs together and fastened them to the table so that I would not roll off. They then strapped each arm to a narrow board at shoulder level that extended at right angles from the table. I could not be more aware of the cross at that moment. Each nurse had their designated assignments and worked away busily without speaking. The sounds of the room seemed to fade, overshadowed by my understanding of what the Lord was allowing to happen in my life. I have always believed that what happens in the natural is a blueprint of what God is doing in the spirit. At that moment I had never felt so close to the word of truth that says we are crucified with Christ (Galatians 2:20). He was taking me on a journey that would surely crucify every worldly way

---

[2] See the Declarations of Truth in Appendix A for more information on cleansing prayers.

and sinful desire that existed in my soul. However, I was not at all fearful and in a sense, I felt the oneness of Him being with me.

As I slowly closed my eyes and rested upon Him, I was not sure what He had prepared for the time I would be under the anaesthetic. I expected to find myself in a beautiful garden, listening to the peaceful chorus, "He walks with me and He talks with me," from the hymn "In the Garden."[3] Instead, I was surprised to hear the lyrics of a familiar battle cry telling me that I was about to go into the enemy's camp and take back what he stole from me! I smiled as I knew the voice of Jesus, my shepherd, in my heart.

Crash! A full tray of surgical instruments fell into a steel sink accompanied by some loud, head-banging music coming from stereo speakers. I was not sure if this was a new technique in helping people emerge from their anaesthetic, but it worked for me. I found myself in a new bed in a cold room designated as "recovery." I was happy to be awake so I could be moved to my assigned room, 443, on the fourth floor. That number held its own promise. In Isaiah 44:3 the Lord's promise is to:

> Pour water on the thirsty land and streams on the dry
> ground; I will pour out my Spirit on your offspring,
> and my blessing on your descendants.

Shortly after I settled in, my family was around my bed, wishing me well. I cannot recall what we spoke about, but I did say my cleansing prayer over the room before slipping off into a deep sleep.

I was aware of nurses coming and going throughout the rest of the day and into the night. Curtains were drawn between the beds and the window blinds closed. Sandra, the night nurse, was born the day after me, and Lesley was the day nurse; the coincidence was difficult to ignore. The Lord had assembled another winning team of Lesley and Sandra. Again, I felt that His commanding hand had chosen the

---

[3]   By C. Austin Miles, 1912.

doctors and the nurses who would care for me. As Sandra did her final check of the room before closing the door to the hallway, I clearly heard the word *Peace*. It may have been from her lips, but sounded more like a whisper from Jesus.

I went home the next day, grateful to have had a good twenty-four hours to recover. Oh, such freedom to be released from the tangled mess of the intravenous needle and its length of hose and hanging bag! I was however, still connected to a small, clear, plastic bulbous container about the size of an avocado that was hooked up to a long tube that in turn was inserted into one of the incisions in my armpit. It would remain attached for a week or so until it became apparent that liquid was no longer draining into it. In the interim I was conscious of the sac, not wanting to lie on top of it or mistakenly pull it out. Lymph nodes are the drainage system for our body, so having had some removed, the tube would temporarily do the job until my body took over. I marvel at how the Lord created our bodies to restore themselves. If a vein is blocked or lymph node is removed, the body just finds an alternate route.

Later that afternoon, I pulled out my Bible devotional calendar and was delighted to see that the daily reading referenced the book of Job. Knowing that Job is perhaps the most famous example of someone enduring pain and suffering, my curiosity led me to look up the reading from the surgery day as well, confident that it would speak directly to my situation and offer welcome words of encouragement.

> I know that my Redeemer lives and that in the end he will stand upon the earth. And after my skin has been destroyed, yet in my flesh I will see God; I myself will see him with my own eyes—I and not another. How my heart yearns within me! (Job 19:25–27)

I could hardly contain my tears as I read this telegram delivered straight from the hand of God. This very scripture had been the basis for a song I had learned during my days at YWAM. On many occasions our team had performed this song by signing the lyrics as a method of reaching out to children who did not speak English. The song recounts the time when God reminds Job of just how big a God He is, by describing the stars in the heavens, the ocean crashing on the shore, His directives to the sun and moon, but most importantly, His victory over death so that we can all have LIFE! With every line of the song, my heart always testified of the truth that *I* know my Redeemer lives, remembering all that He has done for *me*. Long after my mission trips ended, it remained a very personal anthem of thanksgiving and gratefulness, and here He was, quoting it back to me.

We often need a fresh breath of heaven to revive a declaration or scripture that becomes ordinary when we no longer stop to consider its deep and lasting truth. Taking a moment to ponder its current application, I thought about the treatment I was facing—my flesh was surely being destroyed. My declaration of *knowing* Him was on the verge of a closer encounter with the God of the universe. By the time I was finished, I could proclaim a greater level of certainty and faith and declare that my eyes had in fact seen Him.

The previous day's reading confirmed that this life-changing trial would become a testimony as He refined me in the fire.

> When he has tested me, I will come forth as gold (Job 23:10).

Hope was renewed as I believed in this promise, for the gold He created in me would be unlike the gold and silver of this world. It would reflect the glory of the Lord and the love He has for His people.

My roadmap was beginning to open like a scroll before me. I was settling in for the long haul, transitioning through a valley I had never imagined. Erasing all the menial tasks from the whiteboard in my home office, I wrote out the vision—the life-changing purpose that I was to remain fixed upon until the end.

> The mystery that has been kept hidden for ages and generations, but is now disclosed to the saints. To them God has chosen to make known among the Gentiles the glorious riches of this mystery, which is **Christ in you, the hope of glory** (Colossians 1:26-27. Emphasis added).

and

> He who began a good work in you will carry it on to completion until the day of Christ Jesus (Philippians 1:6).

Christ in me, the hope of glory. Yes, this was why God was allowing this suffering. The second promise from Philippians kept me from becoming overwhelmed as I constantly reminded myself that the *Lord* was doing the work within me, and I was just along for the ride. I was confident of the results yet to come, as He is the Master Potter and I am simply the lump of clay in His hands.

> But we have this treasure in jars of clay to show that this all-surpassing power is from God and not from us. We are hard pressed on every side, but not crushed; perplexed, but not in despair; persecuted, but not abandoned; struck down, but not destroyed (2 Corinthians 4:7-9).

We often hear the expression that someone has the patience of Job, but I admire Job in a deeper way, seeing him as a forerunner of sorts who perhaps endured a level of suffering that most of us never experience. He did not have the testimony of one who went before him to draw strength from, so he had to forge his own path. His story continually provides me with encouragement and faith to believe God for the lovely vessel that He will create with His very own hands.

Two weeks later I was scheduled for post-surgery follow-up with the doctor to discuss the pathology report that detailed the characteristics of the tumour and the stage of my cancer. As we had the first appointment of the day, Lesley and I hoped to be in and out fairly quickly, but her experience told her not to count on it. We felt more confident than during our previous visit as we knew where the parking was, what floor we needed to go to, and most importantly, where to find the coffee shop and washrooms! A building that seemed so daunting four weeks ago was no longer intimidating. While walking towards the office, I could not ignore how my life had changed in such a short period of time. Priorities were different and old routines had been completely revamped. We checked in with the nurse and made our way to the waiting area.

I have never understood how a doctor's office can fall behind schedule at 9:00 a.m., but we *still* had to wait. As an organized person, I have always found myself wanting to organize others when I see inefficiencies in their system, particularly if you sit me down in a room with nothing else to do but observe. I suppose it was a clever distraction from the Lord to calm my nerves as I waited.

After being ushered in to see the surgeon, we waited while she perused my file. Rifling through different papers, she pulled out a page and began to read it aloud. After a few moments it became apparent that she was reading from an old report and did not have up-to-date information. My heart sank as this meant another delay while the hospital sent over the latest pathology results. We decided to wait near the reception area, as the atmosphere there was slightly more inviting than sitting atop a hard, paper-lined table in the small, antiseptic-smelling examination room.

Our conversation was limited as we tried not to focus on why we were there. Instead we looked for some distractions in the copious magazines on the table. Each time the fax phone rang we watched with great anticipation, hoping that the next piece of paper would have my name on it. Tossing the magazine I was reading onto the coffee table, I decided that the dead plant on the shelf was slightly more interesting. While looking at the dry, brittle leaves, I could almost hear its plea for water. This doctor came with glowing recommendations, which I may have questioned if I had seen the plant on my last visit!

All efforts to embark upon a mission to find a watering can were suddenly interrupted as I heard a door open just a few feet away. From down the narrow hallway a patient emerged from the examination room, carrying an all-too-familiar plastic folder that contained the same brochures, drawings, information sheets, and book I had received just four weeks before—she must have just been given the news. As she stopped at the front reception desk to make arrangements for her surgery, I felt tears welling up in my eyes. I knew how she felt—the shock of hearing that it has happened to *you*. Just as I had, she seemed to be restraining herself, composed and calm in speech. As she walked out the door and down the hallway, I wanted to run after her and throw my arms around her and tell her that everything was going to be okay. However, I did not move, as I thought, *Who am I to tell her that everything was going to be okay when I was only one month into this ordeal myself?*

Later, the Lord showed me the truth of that moment. For me to have the urge to comfort her meant that I had a life preserver in *my* hands— I had hope!

> Let us hold unswervingly to the hope we profess, for
> he who promised is faithful (Hebrews 10:23).

That single moment proved to be the catalyst for this book, as I knew without any doubt that Jesus was walking this road with me. I had not yet faced chemo or radiation, nor was I familiar with many medical facts or the mortality rate for those diagnosed with breast cancer. All I knew, was that people did die from it. I certainly did not consider myself to be an expert, but even if this journey was unto death, I had hope.

The fax phone rang and all eyes were fixated on the line-by-line printout making its way onto the desk. I was back in the queue to see the doctor.

The staging of cancer is based upon its size, characteristics, and whether or not it has spread to the lymph nodes and other parts of the body. Stage 1 suggests the cancer is in its earliest phase, with no trace of having spread to the lymph nodes. Stages 2 and 3 are for a more organized, larger tumour and Stage 4 reflects a cancer that has spread beyond the breast. Not knowing just how much the Lord had allowed, I was prepared for anything.

I was categorized as having an advanced Stage 2 cancer. The tumour was quite fibrous, measuring fifteen centimetres (six inches) in length with the cancerous portion the size of a golf ball. It had come to within one millimetre of the chest wall, but the lymph nodes were negative for any trace of cancer. One millimetre—that's about the thickness of a piece of cardboard. It had come so close to spreading. My mind drifted off to the day I discovered the lump . . .

On a rainy afternoon in March, I walked to the local quay on my lunch break. It is a great location on the waterfront where you can buy all kinds of fresh produce, foods, coffee, and a variety of goodies. A woman had set up a booth where she advertized energy healing, so I decided that I would sit myself down on the other side of her bamboo screen and do a bit of prayer as I ate my lunch. I prayed at length for her and the fellow she was working on, knowing that the type of power she was tapping into was not of God and was harmful, not healing. I cannot say I felt anything while I was praying, but just believed by faith that I had done something positive to bring truth into someone's life through my heartfelt prayers.

The next morning when I tried to get out of bed I felt excruciating pain in my back. I could hardly move but made it to the floor where I attempted to stretch the muscles. I pulled my knees up to my chest to do some simple exercises but nothing seemed to alleviate the sharp jabs at the base of my spine. As I prayed, the Lord reminded me of my previous day's lunchtime prayer session at the quay. I heard Him whisper, "I did not send you there yesterday." I groaned with regret, realizing I had taken the spiritual battlefield for granted. I had endeavoured to take on something for which I was not trained or fully prepared. I learned a tough lesson about venturing into territory without having the authority or release from the Lord to go. It is HIS battle plan not mine. Although the Lord has defeated the enemy, we must handle the power of God with precision, but most importantly, we must go in His timing, only by His command. I immediately asked for His forgiveness for having engaged in a battle that was not mine, humbled to again realize the effects of a simple mistake. Within a week, I was completely healed from the crippling back pain. It was while I was doing these exercises that I found the lump in my breast. Such a mixed blessing to have found the lump before it had a chance to grow any larger. This was another reminder to me of the Lord's perfect timing. What if I had not decided to have lunch at the waterfront market that day? What if I had not so casually prayed against the powers of darkness on the other side of that bamboo screen? What if the Lord had not let me go? In His wisdom, He used my mistake to reveal the truth. There were so many coincidences that brought me to the discovery of a silent infirmity making its way into my body . . .[4]

I was shocked to learn of the size of the tumour and wondered just how long it had been growing. It was a great relief to have it removed and to hear the good news that I was healing nicely after the surgery. This doctor has a reputation for taking care with a scalpel, making

---

[4]   *Needless Casualties of War* by John Paul Jackson gives us a deeper understanding of this principle.

small incisions that would hardly be noticed. This was, to me, another indication of the Lord's hand of provision and favour.

One huge hurdle had been cleared and I began adapting to the pace of a long distance run. I resigned myself to the reality of losing a year of my life to this hand-to-hand combat. It would be a slow but steady defeat of this disease, a process that would test my endurance and prepare my hands for war. I was beginning to awaken from the spiritual slumber I had been in—a passivity and weariness that hampered my ability to stand firm against the deceptions and assaults of the enemy.

I had three more weeks of recovery before seeing the oncologist (cancer specialist) and was grateful for a time of rest before facing the giant of chemotherapy. I pondered the promise of the Lord about recovering all that is lost or stolen from us.

> I will repay you for the years the locusts have eaten (Joel 2:25).

This may have been a lost year, but I began to believe it would be one of transition and repositioning as I moved from a place of defence to a position of *offence*. No longer would I allow the enemy to mow me down! He had robbed too much from me and now was the time to plunder *his* camp. For all that had been stolen, I was looking for a sevenfold return (Proverbs 6:31) and believed it would come to me in the Lord's timing. For now I needed to steady my gaze upon Him if I hoped to brave the storm, for just beyond the horizon were dark clouds holding the promise of more rain.

chapter four

Our Body: A Gift from God

God's temple is sacred, and you are that temple.
1 CORINTHIANS 3:17

Having sailed for many years, the Lord often gets my attention by using boating analogies when He speaks to me. He reminded me that in any yacht race, a good start is crucial. You must have all your facts including wind speed and direction, tides and currents, and the crew must be ready to work as a team. It is imperative to be prepared for any weather and have a discerning eye to read the sky. Short blasts of wind and rain or squalls may blow through, leaving as quickly as they arrived, while heavier weather can bring on longer, more intense storms. For the race set out before me I was determined to start well, wait out any storms, and finish the course.

During the time of convalescence after surgery I felt a shift occurring. I was beginning to process my diagnosis and come to terms with the fact that I was now unemployed. There was no pay cheque to cover my expenses and no safety net beneath me, as my job was not being held open. As well, I was experiencing the physical limitations of my body. As it was only two weeks since the surgery, my body was still healing and my normal fast pace was slowly being reduced to a gentle crawl. Lymph nodes had been removed from my right arm, so motion was restricted in a limb I had come to take for granted. My only responsibility was to keep exercising it so that it did not gather fluid and swell, developing a condition called lymphedema. The bonus was that the doctor's orders clearly stated, "no heavy lifting and no vacuuming," so I tried to rejoice in the small blessings!

The down time after surgery gave me an opportunity to ponder this season of my life and I began to accept the fact that I was facing cancer as a single woman living alone. Two months prior to my diagnosis I had been comforting a friend who thought she had found a tumour in her neck. I assured her that the Lord would bring helpers if she had to undergo treatment. It was a false alarm for her, but now I found myself recalling the words uttered from my own lips. This had become a critical time for faith to arise.

To look at the circumstances alone would be enough to send anyone into a spiral of deep depression, a demon that I was determined to steer clear of, having fought against it for more than ten years and finally defeating it when I found the Lord. The battlefield within my mind was heating up, so my daily challenge was to respond with the mind of Christ as every fiery dart of the enemy tried to come against me. We are a new creation—old things have passed away, so it was up to me to claim the truth of God's word for my life. I had conquered the enemy of depression, so now I had to walk with certainty in that authority. Just as storm clouds can quickly develop out of nowhere, I have learned that depression too, can sneak in with a simple negative thought.

As we follow Job's progression of emotions throughout his entire ordeal, he went from a man of great confidence, defending himself to his friends, to a man that had simply had enough and wanted the Lord to just end it all. Unsatisfied with the deafening silence from heaven, he protested and cried out to God. Verse after verse, chapter after chapter he uttered his petitions, until finally the voice of God came forth:

> Then the LORD answered Job out of the storm (Job 38:1).

I find it interesting that it was in the *midst of the storm* that he received an answer from on high. As the dark clouds were closing in around *me*, I had just enough faith to believe that the Lord would answer *my* cries in this place, just as He did for His child, Job.

I continued to gather information on everything relating to breast cancer, including what causes it, the treatments and their side effects, and all I could expect to experience over the next few months. So many resources are available that initially it was overwhelming. To compound my frustration, I became surprisingly weary from people's opinions. In an effort to help, everyone became an expert on cancer, offering alternative medicines and regimes that none of them had tried, but all felt would be better than the monster of chemotherapy. The truth was that I needed to hear from the Lord. What would He have me do? Before I could expect to hear an answer from heaven, I realized the need for me to do my homework. In order to make an informed decision with Godly wisdom, I needed to have the facts before me.

Typically I was not someone to read health reports or books about the body because I considered myself to be healthy and frankly, those topics just did not interest me. Unless it was an article about weight loss or the bonuses of eating broccoli (I love broccoli), it would not be on my radar. Now I was learning a whole new language, googling medical terminology on the Internet just to grasp all that was behind this scourge of cancer.

The Lord continued to dazzle me with His brilliance as I learned just how complex the human body is. Simply put, we have billions of cells that are constantly growing, dividing, dying, and rebuilding again. Within each cell is a nucleus, which is where we find our DNA or genes. Abnormal changes in the DNA often cause cells to grow and divide uncontrollably, forming tumours. Cells know to stay in their "assigned places" unless they are cancerous cells that feel free to move around wherever they want, so cancer easily spreads to adjoining organs or through the lymph system into other parts of the body. There are so many factors that can affect our DNA, from the food we eat to the genes we have inherited. Entire books have been written on the cellular makeup of our body and speculation on what causes cancer, but the crux of the matter is that cancer attacks the very foundation of our body, our DNA.

This provided a blueprint for me to see that the Lord was about to turn my world upside down. As the bad DNA cells were being rebuilt into healthy cells within my body, He was strengthening and building up my *spiritual* DNA, right from the cornerstone of its foundation. Understanding this process of restoration and rebuilding takes us right back to the principals of God's kingdom and the transforming power of His cross. Our cornerstone is Jesus and all that is built upon that rock is based upon Godly principles using God's word as the plumb line.

Over the years I have read many great books that helped me to interpret deep mysteries of the Bible. I have also listened to teachings and sermons and attended countless conferences—all part of my effort to run this race with fervency and determination. Sometimes the exciting new levels of revelation had been so intriguing that I tended to complicate the basic message of His gospel: Christ and the cross. I am so grateful for teachers and mentors in my life who constantly reminded me that the foundational truth of the victory that Jesus has won for us is His crucifixion on the hilltop of Calvary outside Jerusalem, the most pivotal moment in history.

In any discussion of Bible-based faith, we must start with an understanding that we live in a fallen world and that all of us are sinners. God's decree has always been that the penalty for sin is death, so from the time we come forth from the womb we owe this debt. However, God loves us so much that His son Jesus took the penalty for *all* of our sins when He died upon the cross. Three days later, He rose from the grave, defeating Satan and freeing us from the grip of Death and Destruction forever. The truth of Calvary's cross continues to offer us freedom from Satan's hold on us and from every kind of sickness and infirmity, simply though our obedience and repentance. Repentance is confessing a sincere desire to change, to turn away from sin; and obedience is walking in the ways of God, trusting in Him enough to obey all His directives.

> Godly sorrow brings repentance that leads to salvation
> and leaves no regret, but worldly sorrow brings death
> (2 Corinthians 7:10).

The Holy Spirit is like a spotlight that shines upon the dark places within us where sin abounds. It exposes where old wounds and disappointments have given place to grief and despair, and where walls have been built around our hearts as a garrison of protection from the hurts of this world. The Holy Spirit is gentle and tender as He works to dismantle the structures that have caused us to be separated from Him and His love. He will only expose to the extent we allow and will never reveal everything at once, as we simply could not handle it. If we harden our heart to His voice, we cannot expect to be released (or delivered) from the clutches of sin. Just as the Israelites kept wandering in the desert, we too, will find ourselves going round and round the same mountain until we are ready to listen to God. As we are convicted of a sin in our lives, our responsibility is to prayerfully take it before the Lord, ask for His forgiveness, and nail it to the cross, believing that the blood that Jesus shed two thousand years ago is still the key to receiving freedom today. The more we learn about who God is, the more we naturally adopt His character, strength, and goodness into our ways. The more we take to the cross in our prayers, the greater transformation we experience.

When God formed us, He gave us a body, a soul, and a spirit. When I invited Jesus into my heart, my spirit became joined to His. As He started to clean me up, my soul began the lifelong journey of sanctification (cleanup) and restoration (healing). The baggage of the world that had loaded me down and settled within my soul needed to be weeded out. Over the years the Holy Spirit has helped me to unpack issues and has taught me the way of the cross, the way that leads to healing and wholeness.

The soul could be referred to as being the "headquarters of self" as it is comprised of our mind, will, and emotions—everything that expresses whom we are. In the process of refinement in becoming more "Christ" like, our intellect is perhaps one of our greatest challenges. A constant battle wages within our mind as we struggle not only to change our unhealthy thought patterns (strongholds), but to believe what is truth—to believe that God's plan for our lives is better than anything we could do without Him.

> "For I know the plans I have for you," declares the LORD, "plans to prosper you and not to harm you, plans to give you hope and a future" (Jeremiah 29:11).

We also struggle to yield to the *will* of God. For years we contend for our independence, then in an effort to draw closer to God, we fight to be released from it. All our bad habits and wild ways do not die easily, presenting us with the constant challenge to crush our will in favour of the higher, more appealing ways of the Lord.

The third component of our soul is our emotions. It is in this place that we often harbour our deepest hurts. From my own experience, I have come to believe that depression is a manifestation of compounded wounds. As every disappointment, regret, and hurt remained locked up, the imposing cloud of sadness became a heavier shroud of darkness. As I began to follow the leading of the Lord to deal with my damaged emotions, the depression finally lifted, making way for the welcome sound of laughter.

I am beginning to accept that we will never attain perfection until we reach heaven. Just when we think we are making headway, the Lord strips away another layer of the onion to expose more truths of the ugliness lurking beneath. However, the process of transformation is liberating as we finally say goodbye to sins that have held us back.

The final resting place for every broken heart is found at the foot of the cross as we exchange all our sorrows for a love that never fails.

Breaking free
After the surgery, I entered into a time of soul searching, seeking a fresh revelation from the Lord about His work within me. He gave me a vision of a very specific sin that had been so deeply buried it had escaped my consciousness. I had lived with its consequences but had never known its presence.

He showed me a picture of myself as a mother, sitting around my dining room table with three little girls—triplets. One represented my soul, another, my spirit, and the last my body. Two were joyfully eating their meal, giggling and content, while the third, my body, was quiet and shy. The Lord allowed me to feel what she was feeling—her sense of loneliness, abandonment, and rejection. She felt unloved and unwanted as her mother never paid much attention to her. If her mother looked her way, it was with shame because of her outer appearance. Her voice was never heard or considered to be important, so she stopped speaking and became quiet and withdrawn in a prison of solitude, knowing that the only reason she was invited along was out of obligation as she was born into the family and the soul and spirit needed somewhere to dwell.

An old door of my heart was pried open, revealing the years of neglect and rejection I had heaped upon my body. I wept as the Lord humbled me with His kindness to reveal this terrible truth. He gently led me down the trail to the entry point of this sin so that it could be pulled out by its very root.

I thought back to when I was a child and watched older girls diet. I learned quickly how to count calories, but never understood how to make calories count. For years I would cut foods and drinks from my diet based on their calories instead of recognizing their nutritional value. I would not drink fruit juice or milk, preferring coffee or water. I did not eat fruit because it had calories. I left rice and potatoes out of my diet entirely, opting instead to have more meat as I was convinced that the protein was good for me. I made so many poor choices and was never satisfied with the way I looked. If I did eat nutritional foods, my motivation was wrong—it was purely for vanity. I would try to lose weight, not to stay healthy, but to look and feel attractive. I cannot recall one day when I felt happy and content with my body. My torso was too short, I was too fat and top-heavy, my nose was too big, my hair too thin, my nails too soft, my legs too heavy, my skin too pale, and my veins too weak. My legs were always covered in bruises that never seemed to heal. Perhaps this was my body's way of complaining to the owner who continually abused it.

The Lord continued to reveal a deeper truth as He reminded me of the story in Luke when the Pharisees wanted Jesus to rebuke His disciples for the loud, joyful praises they were uttering for all the miracles they had seen.

> "I tell you," he [Jesus] replied, "if they keep quiet, the stones will cry out" (Luke 19:40).

Nature responds to its environment and to the Spirit of the Lord, and so it suddenly made sense to me that my body would respond to the rejection it had endured. It had become the product of my negligence. In a heap of tears I repented before the Lord for my lack of nurturing for the body He had blessed me with. Abandoning all sense of decorum, I wrapped my arms around myself and apologized to the body I had ignored for so long. Something beyond my understanding occurred within me as a voice that had been silenced for years could now be heard.

The following morning I opened the refrigerator to grab a bottle of a green health drink that had somehow been buried on the back of a shelf. As I emptied every last nutritious drop into a glass, I sensed a little girl standing beside me with her chin just high enough to reach the countertop. Her tiny hands clapped with glee as she said, "Mommy, Mommy, is that for me?" I then measured out a vitamin and her eyes were wide with excitement. This third child was finally being loved and accepted as part of the family, and God was preparing a temple for His habitation.

chapter five

Deliver Us from Evil

But this kind does not go out except by prayer and fasting.
MATTHEW 17:21

One of the greatest truths about the Lord is that there are no coincidences. He is everywhere and sees everything, so our challenge is to see Him in the midst of our circumstances. Coincidences are usually His way of getting our attention; the great big neon light that says He is trying to show us something. His word says that as we seek Him with all of our heart we will find Him, so if you are looking, you will likely see Him!

It was Mother's Day and our church always has a special program to honour all of the women —whether they are mums or not, it is designated as their special day. I volunteered to make the annual small token gift that each one could take home with them. Hoping to find something that would be memorable, I was inspired to purchase small geranium plants, tie a lovely ribbon around the pot, and write a scripture on a plastic tag that would slip nicely down the inside of the container. Selecting eighty different verses, I trusted that the Lord would match them up to each individual as a personal blessing from Him. Many ladies later expressed their surprise in receiving the verse that they knew was just for them.

I was one of the last people to leave the meeting that morning, but was delighted to see that we had enough gifts that I too could take one home. Anxious to know what the Lord would say to *me*, I eagerly looked for the verse in my plant.

> If you have faith as small as a mustard seed, you can say to this mountain, "Move from here to there" and it will move. Nothing will be impossible for you (Matthew 17:20).

Yes, what a great reminder that I must walk by faith to see this mountain of cancer removed from my path.

The gift I was giving Mum that Sunday was an adorable garden ornament of a little girl holding a basket. The tiny basket looked so empty, that I decided to share the blessing of my baby geranium plant, which was a perfect fit. Mum had such a beautiful garden where she could give our flower a good home. I included the scripture tag so it could be a double blessing and I explained to her where the idea had come from.

A couple of days later, Mum called to say that she felt the scripture was for me. I agreed, but she caught the casualness in my response. She said,

"Did you notice the portion of this verse that is not in the Bible?"

Okay, now I was paying attention—"Huh?"

I pulled out my NIV study Bible and looked up the reference. The plastic card inserted into the plant read, "Matthew 17:21," but I had read Matthew 17:20. Verse twenty-one in this version of the Bible is skipped and is listed only as a footnote. It says:

> But this kind does not go out except by prayer and fasting.

I had missed this the first time around, but in His faithfulness the Lord had orchestrated events to get the message through to me. This verse forms part of the parable Jesus told of the boy who was healed of a demon. Temporarily denying our body food makes a way for the Lord to intervene in power as we offer our complete surrender to Him. After reading this verse, I immediately felt the nudge of the Lord to fast and pray to be fully released from the infirmity of cancer.

Having just completed my lesson on hearing the voice of my body and vowing to care for my temple, I was now embarking on starving it. It seemed an odd move, but I was certain of the call to fast. I was unsure of the duration and type of fast[5] the Lord wanted me to do, so I asked Him to clearly direct me and reveal His perfect timing for it. Knowing that I was approaching the start date of chemotherapy, I was conscious of what my body was about to endure. Now was the time to be building up its strength, not denying it nutrition. If I planned the fast for a later date, I was not sure that I could endure it while trying to cope with the predicted bouts of nausea.

Within a week I had my answer. I had a sense that it was to be a three-day water-only fast, so now I just needed the timeline. One evening I was watching television when an advertisement came on that spoke directly to my heart. A hospital nurse was talking to a patient and said,

"You have cancer."

She went on with all kinds of information and terminology that would be difficult for anyone to follow, sounding as though she was speaking a different language. The camera then panned the room to reveal that the patient was a small child, which reminded me of the parable I had read. The ad was for the Children's Miracle Network Telethon that would be televised the weekend of June 3 and 4. I felt the Lord saying,

Sandra, you are a child with cancer that needs a miracle.

I marked the calendar to begin my fast on Friday, June 2, and finish Sunday evening at 6:00 p.m.

This was perhaps the easiest fast I have ever completed and I

---

5   Mahesh Chavda's book, *The Power Behind Prayer and Fasting,* is an excellent resource for more understanding on this subject.

attribute it to the grace of God. I had very little energy to start; yet He carried me through with no desire for food right up until the final hour. In a switch from my usual fervency for prayer, I found it difficult to pray and recalled what Jesus said about His disciples who struggled to pray during His most crucial hour:

> The spirit is willing, but the body is weak (Mark 14:38).

Still, trusting in the faithfulness of the Lord, I pressed on to do the best I could, believing He would honour my willingness and obedience. As I denied my body food, my ears would be tuned in to clearly hear what the Spirit of the Lord was saying. I was certain of my imminent freedom from all sickness and infirmity as I called upon the name of the Lord. My strategy for prayer was to cover all bases. Just as the parable described the boy being healed, I petitioned heaven to be free of the spirit of cancer and infirmity. I invited others to pray and fast with me as they felt led, as I am a firm believer that more voices make for a greater victory.

> If two of you on earth agree about anything you ask for, it will be done for you by my Father in heaven. For where two or three come together in my name, there am I with them (Matthew 18:19—20).

Intercessors are those who pray to the Lord on your behalf or "intercede" for you. They capture the very nature of the Lord's compassion as they fervently pray to see lost souls saved, wounded hearts restored, and the sick healed. I sought prayer on Sunday morning from a few of these trusted intercessors, and the elders of the church gathered to anoint me with oil and agree in prayer for my complete healing.

> Is any one of you sick? He should call the elders of the church to pray over him and anoint him with oil in the name of the Lord. And the prayer offered in faith

will make the sick person well; the Lord will raise
him up. If he has sinned, he will be forgiven (James
5:14—15).

By "coincidence" that Sunday was Pentecost Sunday, as well as the
Global Day of Prayer. Although millions of people were not praying
specifically for Sandra Crawford, I felt a great outpouring of the Holy
Spirit and imagined an open window in heaven receiving the fervent
prayers of the saints.

The following evening I attended a prayer mentoring class where
we typically would have a teaching followed by intercessory prayer.
That night the Holy Spirit took us in a different direction than our
normal meetings. The leaders were always sensitive to the leading of
the Lord, yielding their agendas in favour of His will. Nearly forty of
us were silently waiting upon the Lord that night, all with an anxious
anticipation of what He would do.

As I quieted my soul, in the stillness I felt the Lord approaching.
It was as though a slight breeze was building into a stronger fresh
wind. In my spirit I heard one sentence:

Sandra, I chose you for my Son.

The Lord left me to meditate on this single truth before He spoke
again.

You did not choose me, but I chose you (John 15:16).

A few moments later, another scripture dropped into my spirit:

> From the beginning God chose you to be saved through
> the sanctifying work of the Spirit and through belief
> in the truth (2 Thessalonians 2:13).

Jesus chose many to be part of His kingdom. Together, we all make
up one body, the bride that He will come for when He returns. I
sensed He was personalizing this for me so I would have a deeper
understanding of His love. He was calling me by name, which forced
my heart to hear the truth, confirming what my mind already knew.
When someone addresses me by name, I tend to pay more attention

and offer a response. With the room fading away around me, I seemed to step into this truth simply through my faith to believe. In my spirit, I again heard, *Sandra, I chose you for my Son.* The repeated call kept me from losing momentum. With trepidation I continued to wade deeper into a place in the Spirit where I had never ventured before. The word of God washed over me, obliterating fear and releasing faith.

> Deep calls to deep in the roar of your waterfalls; all
> your waves and breakers have swept over me (Psalm
> 42:7).

His wave became a powerful force that I could not contain. As He continued to sweep over me I felt Him touch me to the very core, His power causing my knees to buckle as I gasped to catch my breath. My body gave up any struggle to fight the hand of God as He filled me to overflowing with His very essence. It felt like liquid love was being poured into me—weighty oil that was lasting and pure. As I lay sprawled out across the altar, this wave began to ebb as I continued to process all that had just occurred. My breathing settled back to a normal rate when a few moments later I again felt the breath of wind pick up. He swept over me again and again, seeming to pour out as much as I could endure. Just when I thought He was finished, the wave would knock me down once more. I felt I was in the presence of the Holy Trinity—my heavenly Father, Jesus His Son, and the Holy Spirit of God. They surrounded me on every side and lingered—a promise that they were not leaving, nor would they *ever* leave. This encounter cemented my current level of faith and gave me a higher rock to reach for—a new dimension. My three-day fast emptied me in preparation for this infilling from the throne room of heaven.

The substance of courage

At this juncture I faced a critical decision. The tumour had been removed, and through prayer I had been released from all infirmities. The extreme fatigue I had experienced over the past few months lifted, as my body was no longer trying to fight the cancer, but there was no way to perform a medical test that would confirm my healing. Would my faith wane if I went through the rigorous chemotherapy that had been prescribed? Did I doubt the hand of God that I believed with certainty had reached down from heaven and touched me? I resisted the temptation to listen to the voice of many who would say, "You are healed. Carry on with your life." This was a desirable path, as I could resume my daily activities having endured very little disruption or pain. However, when I am unsettled and lacking the peace of the Lord, I know that I have not found His will. The restlessness within my soul pointed to the truth that I was trying to find an escape route out of this valley of fear about the treatment. Everything I had heard about the whole process of chemotherapy scared me, but courage caused me to seek the Lord in this hour for *His* answer. I could have made a snap decision, skirting the issue and quickly moving on, but the substance of courage is to believe you can overcome fear.

> Be on your guard; stand firm in the faith; be men of courage; be strong (1 Corinthians 16:13).

Psalm 91 speaks of the protection of God that we experience as we rest and trust in Him.

> He who dwells in the shelter of the Most High will rest in the shadow of the Almighty. I will say of the LORD, "He is my refuge and my fortress, my God, in whom I trust" (vv.1—2).

As I stood at this crossroad I waited safely under the shadow of His wings, not looking into the face of fear, but fixing my gaze upon Jesus the shepherd, awaiting His directive.

chapter six

Spilled Milk

Cast all your anxiety on him because he cares for you.
1 PETER 5:7

A good commander sends a reconnaissance team out ahead of his troops to survey the land. Based on this "intel," he formulates a strategic plan of attack. My first visit to the cancer agency was my reconnaissance mission to gather the facts specific to my case before deciding what my next move would be. I was not committed to chemotherapy yet, so I could still decline treatment.

The British Columbia Cancer Agency has more than one site in the province. I was directed to meet with an oncologist at the Vancouver location, which is located on the corner of *Ash* Street and *10th* Avenue. The still small voice of the Lord reminded me of His promise from Isaiah 61 to give me "a crown of beauty for ashes." Throughout the scripture, ten often represents the number for trials and testing; turning or completion. The ever-present hand of the Lord was leading me.

I entered the lobby area alone while Lesley parked the car. It was a blessing to walk in on my own as I immediately became aware of a spiritual heaviness that may have slipped by unnoticed had I been engaged in conversation. Having experienced this only a few times in the past couple of years, the sense of a spiritual mixture was recognizable, instantly causing my spirit to stand to attention. As I was handed a clipboard, I quietly prayed my usual prayers of covering and protection over us. Working my way over to the waiting area, I asked the Lord to increase my discernment so that I could better understand this complex spiritual atmosphere. The enemy is always prowling around seeking whom he may destroy, so my stance is to be prepared and on alert, particularly in new territory.

Completing the first round of paperwork, I returned it to the reception desk and took a seat in the waiting area. Lesley and I had been advised that our meeting could take a couple of hours, so we came prepared with our questions, comparing notes at every available moment. Based on the research I had done, I semi-expected to hear that the recommendations for treatment would be six months of chemotherapy followed by five weeks of radiation. Our discussion was so much more, as though we had unknowingly enrolled in a crash course in oncology only days after learning the definition of the word.

The building was well appointed in every area, yet not revealing its age in any of the usual spots. The carpet and chairs are obvious indications of the level of maintenance in any hospital, and here the environment was clean, well kept, and welcoming. Even the usual out of date magazines had been replaced by fairly recent publications. It was a pleasant surprise to see how efficiently each department ran, the attention to detail reflecting years of experience. Every effort had been made to put people at ease. Jigsaw puzzles sat on tables in various stages of completion at every cluster of chairs; beautiful handmade quilts hung in foyers, and serene paintings adorned the hallways. The staff and volunteers generally were courteous and friendly, passing through the lobby periodically with trolleys of water, tea, and cookies.

A nurse summoned us into a small examination room, where she interviewed me, completing more forms, including a comprehensive medical history. She took down the usual details of height and weight and worked her way through the history of every decade of my life. Painting a clear picture of the patient helps to find answers about the cause and spread of cancer and to assess what treatment is best for each situation. As we eagerly asked our questions, the quiet-mannered nurse seemed to become a little overwhelmed and thrown off-task. Our confidence began to slide when we did not get definitive answers, unaware that the questions and concerns we bombarded her with would all be handled in due course. The consultation process seemed to take forever and we had not even *seen* a doctor yet. Eventually round one was completed and we were left to wait again.

A new face entered the room and announced that she was an intern working with the doctor and that she would begin the exam. She politely went over the answers I had given to the nurse, filling in specific details about how I had discovered the cancer and the course of action that had been taken from meeting with my general practitioner, to the biopsies, mammogram, and surgery. Reliving the last few weeks was not pleasant, but necessary in order to pass the baton to a new doctor.

She noted my line of work, my general health, past and present; my complete medical and surgical history, sleep patterns, social history, and any other details that could be classified as pertinent, including health issues from previous generations in my family. A physical exam followed from head to toe, feeling for any new lumps or abnormalities. She listened to my heart, took a blood pressure reading, and closely inspected the area where the tumour and lymph nodes had been removed. Round two was completed, and we waited once again.

A third new face entered the room—the doctor. Just as we respond at a show when the main act finally hits the stage, we were so excited to see her that we nearly jumped to our feet with a round of exuberant applause! Her intern followed close behind, so we had a full house in the examination room. Dr. Abrams[6] is a confident woman whose commanding presence immediately put me at ease. After spending

---

6   Doctor's name has been changed for privacy.

two hours talking to a nurse and a timid young intern who did not move at the same speed as my overactive brain, it was comforting to have a big gun arrive. She briefly looked over the notes and then asked some pointed questions to complete the paperwork and gain a full understanding of who Sandra Crawford was. For the first time I felt like someone had acknowledged the *person* behind the treatment, which was a refreshing and welcome change.

Dr. Abrams then took out a large notepad and methodically walked us through what amounted to Oncology 101, using my pathology results for the case study. She began by stating that the goal was to cure the operable cancer in the breast. Then she presented documented statistics on those patients that chose to use chemotherapy and radiation treatments, carefully laying out the risks involved and the drug protocols. Timelines and detailed diagrams of the expected side effects for each leg of the journey ensured that I had a clear picture of the process before making a decision. Having taught many people throughout my own career, I appreciated her ability to communicate such a difficult subject to two novices. Since *she* was drawing the charts and writing the notes, I could concentrate on absorbing the barrage of information. In addition to the basic understanding of treatment, she addressed three areas that were specific to my case.

She noted from my medical history that I had been previously diagnosed with depression, a concern as chemotherapy drugs affect the serotonin levels in the body, which for me would most assuredly mean a trip down a familiar path. Her concern centred on whether or not I could take it and emerge from the treatment without a black cloud over my head. Recounting my experiences with depression, I attributed my complete recovery to the hand of God. I expected to see a blank look on her face and the usual discomfort most people display when the name of Jesus is mentioned. Surprisingly, she asked me to continue, and so of course I proceeded to tell her more about my beloved Jesus! She seemed satisfied as I spoke with conviction and certainty of my victory over the darkness of depression. I was doubly blessed by her compassion to hear me out as I realized that she needed to be convinced of the truth of my testimony. A weak declaration of my faith and belief in God and His unfailing love would not slip by unnoticed. Prescribing chemotherapy is a serious affair with life-threatening side effects and Dr. Abrams showed attentiveness and discernment as I stated my case.

The second subject for discussion concerned my desire for children. I was unprepared for this topic, as its relevance to my treatment had not occurred to me. Chemotherapy for a woman of my age would inevitably bring on premature menopause, so I was suddenly faced with the realization that an unfulfilled desire buried deep within me may never come to pass. The hope of having children had gradually waned over the years and now it was slipping out of reach. Until then, I had not consciously dealt with this issue, choosing instead to push it aside. My choice for treatment could close that door of hope permanently. The reality of never carrying a baby in my womb brought tears to my eyes, but I knew that if I let just one tear escape a dam would burst. Wrestling with the harsh truth that had just been delivered, I held my emotions in with every bit of strength I could muster.

Finally, the doctor advised us that a lymph node that had been removed at the chest wall had been found to be cancerous. This had been missed during the final consultation with the surgeon, so the news came as quite a surprise. I felt as if I had just been dealt a double blow—cancer may have spread to other parts of my body. To rule out this possibility, Dr. Abrams gave me requisitions for a new round of tests. A bone scan would be required for my whole body. To check my core organs, she ordered an ultrasound on my liver, gall bladder, kidneys, and stomach area. Lastly, a chest x-ray would reveal if there was any cancer in my lungs.

Dr. Abrams had great compassion as she reported these findings, often pausing to allow us time to catch our breath. Her professionalism was evident in all aspects of her care for me. Without even knowing her, I felt I had a friend on my side as she pressed on to outline the next nine months of my life as she worked to save it.

For each chemotherapy drug selected for my protocol, she gave me a complete written synopsis that outlined the description of the drug, the treatment plan, instructions for the patient, and possible side effects. Following each treatment of chemotherapy, my white blood count would drop right off the chart. If all went well, three weeks later it would bounce back up and I would be ready for the next round. However, if it did not, I would require an injection to enhance and accelerate the development of cells.

As a responsible physician she was obliged to explain the side effects, whether minimal or extreme. After hearing the list, I felt as if I had just walked into a shower of enemy arrows labelled "fear" that were targeting my mind. I expected to hear about some of the more common, well-known side effects associated with cancer patients, such as nausea, vomiting, and hair loss. However, others came from nowhere and made a direct hit: Possible heart failure, tissue injury, infection, weight gain, mouth sores, change in taste, joint pain, and fatigue—the list seemed endless. A glazed look came over my eyes, as I knew I had gone well past my capacity to endure this onslaught.

As we approached the end of our meeting I felt mentally exhausted but educated. At no time was I rushed or intimidated, but instead I felt respected as an individual rather than a number. Dr. Abrams handed me prescriptions for all the drugs that I would need to combat the side effects—drugs for the drugs. I tucked them into my folder and after saying my goodbyes, walked back to the car in silence with Lesley by my side. We had been in the clinic for more than four hours.

Everything seemed a blur as I climbed into the car and so I was grateful to have someone else driving whom I could talk to. We rehashed much of what was said, doing our best to establish the facts. I am not sure when I arrived home, but I knew with certainty I wanted to run to the cross. Without words, I simply cried out from my heart for the comforting arms of Jesus. Having nothing left within me to form even the simplest of prayers I slipped off into a deep sleep, hoping that this nightmare would end by the morning.

The next day, a heaviness remained as sleep had not erased my burden—I had yet to carry it to the cross. I have learned that fatigue can often be a sign of carrying a heavy load, so I proceeded to do some spiritual housecleaning. My fireplace is such a warm, welcoming spot in my home and for that reason it has been my favourite meeting place with the Lord. On this day I longed for His presence and reached for my Jewish prayer shawl that has always been precious to me. Since visiting Israel, I have come to love and appreciate the Jewish culture and customs, stirring an even deeper love in my heart for Jesus. These prayer shawls are traditionally draped over the head of those engaging in prayer to the Holy One of Israel, but on that morning, I laid it out across the hearth as a makeshift altar in preparation for my time of prayer before the throne of heaven.

First Peter 5:7 says, "Cast all your anxiety on Him because He cares for you." Instead of just speaking the words, I decided to make it a physical act of casting my burdens upon Him. I pulled my backpack out of the hall cupboard and began the hunt to gather every last piece of paper from every room in my home that related to the cancer. Every book, pamphlet, appointment card, drug protocol and prescription was tossed into the pack. Sitting before the Lord, under the guidance of the Holy Spirit, I wrote on separate pieces of paper every one of my anxieties and worries, whether it was a fear about the cancer or simply my fears of the future. The pile of papers grew as I wrote furiously, identifying fears about the treatment and the side effects, fear of the cancer having spread, a stomach-churning nausea of the ugliness of the whole episode, a resentment that I was seeing more of my life stolen by the enemy, and the reality of the huge mountain before me. This process proved to be revealing as the Holy Spirit continued to highlight fears and some surprising burdens, including a fear of needles.

Many years ago I had been traumatized by a simple blood test. On that day the nurse had been clearly agitated by my polite request to take the blood from a vein in my hand, perhaps feeling that I was trying to tell her how to do her job. Too often I had become a pincushion for lab techies who wanted to prove their skill in being the first to find a vein in my arm on the first try. This nurse's gruff manner with me resulted in bruises all over my arm from her unsuccessful efforts to find a vein. I had not realized that I was carrying this fear of needles, and now I was scheduled to be poked at least forty times over the next nine months.

Another burden I carried was for someone I loved dearly. I had always tried to encourage and build them up, particularly after they suffered great loss or faced difficult challenges of their own. The Lord revealed to me that I once again fell into the role as being the burden-bearer, taking responsibility for others' sorrow as they stood on the sidelines watching me go through this bout with cancer. In this situation, I had convinced myself that my faith would be sufficient for both of us, and that maybe they too, would fall in love with my beloved Jesus. The Lord reminded me that it is His role to carry their burdens, not mine.

During this time in prayer, the Lord also revealed a greater understanding of the magnitude of this battle and my responsibility to have other strong prayer warriors standing with me. He reminded me of an incident that occurred a few days before, when I was scheduled for an exam at a nearby hospital. As an independent, single woman, I was confident in my ability to handle it alone so did not feel it was necessary to ask anyone to accompany me. While parking the car, I recalled that the last time I was at that hospital, in that parking lot, was when someone I deeply cared about passed away. Fighting back tears over their lost life, I realized that I did in fact need support to get through the next few hours. I felt loneliness creeping in as I walked down the hallway towards the information desk. The Lord's direction was gentle as He impressed upon me the importance of having solid prayer partners to cover me at every turn. I could not fight this battle alone and did not know what could be lurking around the next corner. Repenting for my pride and self-reliance, I learned a valuable lesson and from that point on, recruited willing, trained soldiers who would stand with me in the tough times.

During this simple act of writing out my fears and releasing my burdens at the foot of the cross, it amazed me to see the depth to which the Holy Spirit had reached, revealing some profound truths that were well beyond my conscious mind. The last one to be uncovered was a surprisingly deep resentment towards my forefathers.

I believe curses are handed down from one generation to the next (Exodus 34:7), and that sin perpetuates itself from generation to generation if we open a door to it. In the on-going process of sanctification I have gone before the Lord to repent on behalf of my forefathers more times than I could count, which ultimately brought freedom to me and the generations that follow. This time, however, the diagnosis of cancer hit me so hard that the weariness nearly brought me to a place of defeat—that I just could not do it anymore. Instead of blaming the enemy, I blamed my ancestors. I wept with desperation as I asked why *they* did not answer the call of the Lord.

Why did they not follow a life of righteousness to give me a blessed heritage instead of one with so much baggage? Why did they blaspheme the God who loved them and turn their backs on the Jesus I love? Why did I have the weight of finding the truth and carrying the sin to the cross?

In my selfishness I could only weep for my problems and myself instead of seeing that it was only by God's grace that I was rescued at all. In my brokenness I reached a deeper appreciation for the fear of the Lord as I grasped how close I had come to spending a lost eternity in hell. I experienced a deep forgiveness for my ancestors as I chose to repent for their sins. My heart immediately became saturated with passion to see the ones I love be snatched from the fire.

My backpack was heavy as I brought it before the Lord, laying it upon the prayer shawl. Already, I was feeling lighter as I symbolically released it into God's hands. I prayed through every last item, repenting for my fears, forgiving all who hurt me, and forgiving myself for my mistakes. My final words were to reject every fiery dart from the enemy. When I had finished, the peace of the Lord was tangible. In silence I waited upon Him for direction and He faithfully responded with a very clear vision.

He showed me a picture of a glass of milk that had been spilled. Surgery removed the glass (the tumour), but the milk needed to be mopped up. I knew that through this simple picture the Lord was directing me to proceed with chemotherapy to remove any cancerous cells that remained in my body. I had my answer.

If I had attempted to hear the Lord's directive before the trek to the cross, before the act of removing the burdens and fears, my judgment definitely would have been clouded. Fear has a way of moulding an undesirable action into something completely different, easily convincing you that the path of least resistance is the right way to go. Previously, my filter had been clogged with fear, so chances are I would not have been receptive to the idea of chemotherapy, had I not understood the need to mop up the mess. He gave me the courage to stop, ask the question, and wait for a response.

Nobody knows why the Lord chooses to heal some by one touch of His hand while allowing others to endure suffering as they reach for their healing. For me, I was beginning to see that there were so many more reasons for my trials than just to be healed. The deeper work was to strip away old ways, old wounds, and find hope for my future.

> Blessed is the man who perseveres under trial, because when he has stood the test, he will receive the crown of life that God has promised to those who love him (James 1:12).

On the journey to abundant life, I needed to trust and believe in the one who holds all things in His hands. His ways are higher than our ways, so my confession of trust in Him was about to be thrust into the refiner's fire to be tested.

His peace is my barometer for decisions, so having surrendered all my burdens, my fears, and concerns to Him, my heart was comforted once again to know that I was on my way to being restored. My instructions were clear. Raising my sails, I set a course embarking upon the next leg of the journey. I braced myself for the next cycle of tests and filled all the prescriptions, ready for round one of chemo.

chapter seven

In the Cocoon

Let us fix our eyes on Jesus.

HEBREWS 12:2

I have often wondered if a caterpillar knows when it is about to become a butterfly. When it spins that silky skin, does it understand the transformation that is going to take place? Is it even aware that this is one of the spectacular wonders of nature? I consider it a lovely surprise when I spot one of these delicate creatures and I seem to find them in the most unusual places. When I was in India, two butterflies were so bold as to flutter into the midst of us when we were standing in the street. There we were in a poverty-stricken country feeling grimy from the combination of road dirt, pollution, and sweat, and a beautiful butterfly landed on Mum's hand. It stayed for the longest time, seeming to show off its colourful wings as it gently waved them before us. Proudly displaying their vibrant colors, I am sure there comes a point when they are grateful for the long process in the cocoon—that it has all been worth it. But still, that "in between" stage must be so difficult for this tiny creature. Perhaps there are days in the cocoon when it asks, "Am I still a caterpillar today?" Even when it is ready to emerge, the wings are fragile and weak, not yet ready for flight. Do they struggle with impatience as we do?

As I prepared for my own metamorphosis, I continued to walk closely with the Lord, praising Him for all that He would accomplish. Each time I entered a hospital for tests, I knew He was with me. I encountered much hopelessness and fear in other patients around me and realized how blessed I was to know Jesus and the tender love He has for me. He had patiently taught me how to face my fears, overcome them, and stand firm, assured of victory.

One of my greatest breakthroughs came when I realized how much I tried to do in my own strength by striving in so many areas of my life. I had long heeded the adages, "Time heals all wounds," and "Grin and bear it." However, by doing so I ignored conflicts, questions, and fears in the hope that they would go away as I kept that stiff upper lip. Eventually problems did fade, but they were not forgotten. I believe that depression is a manifestation of many unresolved issues locked away behind a veil of darkness; its depth in direct proportion to the number and nature of the issues involved. The longer they stay hidden, the greater courage it takes to expose them. With nothing left to lose, I gave the Lord complete freedom to reveal all that was lurking in the shadows.

As the metamorphosis continued, the word of truth breathed new life into me. Faith and hope moved me from a place of floundering to a place of strength and confidence where I could overcome every challenge.

His joy is my strength

Hospitals and waiting rooms became a regular regime for me as I systematically worked through each of the additional tests. Most medical-related anxieties had long faded away and I felt little or no trace of intimidation each time I arrived at the hospital. Tests now seemed routine as I had come to appreciate the healthcare system and its benefits. The chest x-ray and ultrasound were finished and one final test remained: the bone scan.

The whole procedure for the bone scan fascinated me, as did the term "nuclear" medicine. I would be injected with a radioactive tracing substance and then return a few hours later when I would be "hot" and ready for scanning under the high-resolution camera. My experience is that when the Lord sets us free from sin, we are often tested, usually within hours or days of our closing prayer. With the bone scan, my opportunity arrived to be tested on my fear of needles. I half-expected the poison arrows of possible side effects to be hurled my way and sure enough, at the beginning of my appointment the nurse began to list the many hazards and warnings associated with this type of medical test.

"If the needle does not hit the vein, it will burn your flesh." *Okay, deep breath.*

"Are you sure you don't feel a burning sensation in your flesh?" the nurse asked. She then proceeded to pull the needle back and forth a couple of times to make sure she was successful in hitting the vein without going out the other side. She may have struck the vein, but I would not let her strike a nerve! I was so elated at having conquered my fear of needles, that the three shades of bruising taking form on my hand did not faze me.

A few hours later I was lying on a conveyor belt, slowly entering a large, daunting chamber that scanned me from head to toe (not unlike the scan that the Holy Spirit was simultaneously performing in me.) Deciding to take an active part in the tests, I asked the technician what she looks for on the slide.

"The nuclear liquid shows up on the screen as a bright neon light. An organized collection of fluid in any one region indicates the presence of cancerous cells."

When my scan was complete, I asked to see the computerized image. I was immediately drawn to a neon cluster in the abdominal area. Before fear had a chance to show its ugly face, I calmly asked, "What's all that?"

She replied, "Oh, that's just the radioactive fluid that has been flushed through to your bladder."

Whew! Knowing that there were no other places on the images to worry about, I took a moment to look at my skeleton—God's amazing handiwork. I giggled when I looked closely as without flesh, it appears that the skeleton is smiling. Pleased to discover that I have happy bones, I pondered on the truth that we really can be very happy without our "flesh!"

Immediately following the bone scan, I drove down to Washington State to attend a Christian conference. Still recovering from surgery, I was weak but grateful to still have the ability to drive. I felt so alive as I took in the spectacular scenery of the Pacific Northwest on such a beautiful summer's day. It was a welcome change from the confinement of a hospital room or doctor's office. After a ten-minute wait in the line-up at the border, I was greeted by a series of alarms as I pulled up to the U.S. customs booth. The officer politely asked me where I was going and then directed me to park for an inspection. Apparently their monitoring equipment had identified me as transporting nuclear goods! As I entered their office I smiled and thought to myself, *At least they won't make me wear a hospital gown.* Thankfully, I had with me a letter from the hospital stating that I had recently participated in medical testing that used radioisotopes. Nevertheless they quickly moved me to a separate section of the building where an official appeared with a testing kit—a monitor that measured and displayed my radioactivity. The officer gingerly walked towards me and then, reading the display, abruptly stopped.

"Whoa!" he said as he began to back away from me.

Suppressing a laugh I replied, "Am I to assume you don't want to give me a hug?"—a little comic relief to lighten an otherwise embarrassing moment! After confirming the validity of the hospital's letter and performing a thorough search of my car, they let me proceed.

It can be dark in a cocoon
God, in His faithfulness, sent me to this conference to hear some timely instruction. Just as our pastors listen to the voice of the Good Shepherd to lead the flock, conferences, when orchestrated by the Lord, are perfectly timed to reveal a greater work He is doing in His church or the nation. This particular conference generated much discussion on transformation. I was reminded that everything in Creation begins in the dark.

> In the beginning God created the heavens and the
> earth. Now the earth was formless and empty, darkness
> was over the surface of the deep, and the Spirit of God
> was hovering over the waters (Genesis 1:1–2).

Also, consider a baby in a dark womb, seeds buried in the soil, and an unborn chick inside a dark egg. As God is working in us, it is inevitable that we will go through places of darkness. We often will not understand what is going on, nor will we know when it will end. In these times we must trust in what we already know to be the faithful character of God and hold fast to His promises.

> Not that I have already obtained all this, or have
> already been made perfect, but I press on to take
> hold of that for which Christ Jesus took hold of me
> (Philippians 3:12).

When we have endured suffering, a new door will be opened to us and a greater level of authority will be granted. Jesus came to bring people *in*, not to shut them out. The bright light of His holiness exposes our sin so we can be free from it, not so that we fall under condemnation. The greater liberty we experience, the higher level of God's glory and power can be experienced. It is like climbing a staircase—we are drawn to the light that continues to get brighter with each step.

For now, I had to find contentment while being set apart for His work within me. In an attempt to maintain some sense of normalcy, I attended prayer meetings, but was quickly convicted by the voice of the Lord calling me back to meet with Him in solitude. I felt like a warrior that had been called off the battlefield, laying my weapons down and removing my well-worn armour. In my saddened heart I asked, *Have I failed in my assignment or let down my guard?* He showed me that my involvement in ministries was taking my focus away from the task at hand. They had become a distraction when I needed to concentrate on all that He was doing in me. My complete commitment to this "project" was to be my number one priority. In obedience I withdrew from every ministry I was involved in so that I could meet with Him in the cleft of the rock, just as Moses did when he climbed the mountain to be alone with God.

Not knowing how much energy I would have when chemotherapy began, I did as much preparation in advance as possible. I made a large batch of "Sandra's Fabulous Broccoli Soup," freezing it in small servings, and stocked up on individual packages of crackers and other treatment-friendly foods. Every last piece of laundry was washed and put away, my apartment was cleaned, bills were paid, and all my friends had been contacted with the latest update. With no other excuses permitting me to procrastinate, one last job remained: wig shopping. Facing my inevitable hair loss was something I tried to ignore, so I waited as long as I could before venturing out to make this purchase. I was surprised to learn that few shops in Vancouver specialize in wigs, but I eventually found one that sounded like the Lord's choice—"Butterflies."

I have never worn a wig and the prospect of having to because I would be bald did not make it any easier. A friend had agreed to meet me at the shop to help me make the best of a sad and uncomfortable situation. I hoped we could laugh and have fun as we experimented with different colours and styles. As it turned out, she got lost on the way, which meant I had nearly half an hour to look around the shop on my own. Perusing the selection available, I picked up a few samples but was not too enthused about trying any of them on, particularly as they wanted to charge me five dollars for the privilege. Then I began to question if I was buying a wig for me, or simply to put others at ease—those who did not know how to respond to my bald head. After deliberating for thirty minutes I decided against a wig, feeling that it represented a need or desire to cover my deep, hidden shame and that wearing one would merely mask what the Lord was doing in me. The unexpected delay of my friend had been the Lord's hand, for if I had walked into the shop with her, I am not sure I would have had this revelation. Her compliments and words of encouragement may have silenced the still small voice that said this was not for me.

Although I was not sure how I would handle losing my hair, I was certain of the freedom I experienced with my decision that day as I "fluttered" out of the shop.

Adorned in splendour

Even though I had hardly started this journey, I felt a longing to talk to someone who understood all that I was going through. Well-wishers were offering so many opinions but few comprehended the fragility of the emotional struggle. Support groups did not appeal to me because members generally depend on one another for strength instead of finding it in Jesus. This was not a time for me to challenge their way of doing things, defend my faith, or convince them of God's love. I just needed a helping hand from someone who already knew of His mercy and grace and could encourage me in this hour.

Many years earlier I had briefly met a woman, similar in age to me, who attended my mum's church. Our paths had crossed just about the time she was going through her own battle with breast cancer. One evening I stood in church a few rows behind her, on the opposite side of the aisle. To avoid getting distracted during the time of worship, I usually close my eyes, turning my attention to the Lord. However this time, something alerted me to open my eyes. My gaze was drawn towards her as I witnessed her arms reaching towards heaven and her gentle voice singing unto the Lord. For some reason, this scene was indelibly sealed in my heart as a picture of grace and thanksgiving. In the midst of her struggle, she worshiped the Lord with sincerity and passion. Now, many years later, she was happy to meet with me and share her experiences. The Lord, who exists outside of time, had linked two women who faced the same demon. Often we think our responsibility when becoming a Christian is to run off to the mission fields of developing countries. However, one of the greatest needs is to disciple the spiritually hungry and uplift the battle weary, many of whom can be found in our backyard.

Elizabeth was candid as she shared the intimate struggles and practical aspects of her treatment. What she remembered most was that she too grew into a greater level of intimacy with the Lord than she had ever experienced before. This confirmed that I needed to give myself permission to shut out the rest of the world and sit at the feet of Jesus for a season. Others may find comfort and strength in visiting with family and friends, but I was content to rest in the comfort of His embrace. He is the only one who truly knows the tears and pain of this kind of suffering and can provide the remedy of peace in its midst. He longs for us to have that passionate first love restored in our hearts if it has grown lukewarm, reminding us of the heights from which we have fallen and restoring our hope for tomorrow.

"Clothe yourself with splendour and strength" was a phrase I heard many times in the week leading up to the first chemo treatment, so I asked Him to give me more understanding of what it meant. In the Bible, clothes and jewels often symbolize strength and joy, so I began to research the biblical promises that referenced these two items. They often appear when the Lord describes His bride and how He adorns her with jewels.

One morning my devotional reading took me to the story of Samson and Delilah (see Judges 16). I found it interesting that his strength was in his hair, and I was on the verge of losing mine. As I continued reading, I discovered that Samson killed nearly three times as many enemies in his death than he did throughout his whole life. Although there was a time when he was completely stripped of his power, he learned a very hard lesson about the powers of sin. It changed the course of his life, but in the end, the Lord redeemed what was lost by allowing his final feat to be spectacular. I believe this story was a promise to me of what was yet to come. Just like Samson, I made mistakes in my life that brought consequences. If I had lived a Godly life from the beginning, perhaps I would have had the children I desired. In the weeks to come as I watched my hair fall out and witnessed my strength being sucked out of me, I held onto the hope that God would restore me to a level of strength far beyond anything I had ever known.

The story of Job again came back to me as I was reminded of the double portion he received after enduring his trial.

After Job had prayed for his friends, the LORD made him prosperous again and gave him twice as much as he had before (Job 42:10).

The LORD blessed the latter part of Job's life more than the first (Job 42:12).

The apostle Paul spoke of his sufferings in his letter to the Corinthians.

But I will not boast about myself, except about my weaknesses (2 Corinthians 12:5).

But he [Jesus] said to me, "My grace is sufficient for you, for my power is made perfect in weakness." Therefore I will boast all the more gladly about my weaknesses, so that Christ's power may rest on me (2 Corinthians 12:9).

These words of hope became precious promises that I would hold onto when confined by the walls of my cocoon. As I prepared to lose my strength, I believed that one day I would emerge as a gorgeous butterfly, adorned with a beauty that could only be attributed as having come from the hand of the Lord.

chapter eight

Counterstrike

Be strong in the Lord and the power of His might.
EPHESIANS 6:10 NKJV®

The morning of my first chemo treatment began like any other day. After breakfast, I cleared away the dishes and then packed my hospital kit bag, complete with crackers, pills, and a portable CD player. As I absentmindedly completed my routine, my thoughts could not escape what lay ahead. Stepping into the shower, I stood beneath the warm spray, silently praying to the Lord, asking for His comfort and wisdom. In quiet contemplation, I sensed the subtle stirring of fear—a fear of the unknown. Knowing it often rides the coattails of my trials, I had little confidence in my own abilities to overcome it and so searched for courage in the secret place of the Lord.

After shampooing my hair I reached for the bottle of conditioner from the rack. As I squeezed the tube into the palm of my hand it hit me: three weeks from now my hair will be gone. Split ends seemed like such a trivial concern. Overwhelmed, I quickly recognized the enemy's tactic to bury me beneath anxieties and worries of the future, so I re-focused my attention on the present. The Lord was teaching me to take one day at a time, a discipline that has proved to be an ongoing struggle.

> Therefore do not worry about tomorrow, for tomorrow
> will worry about itself. Each day has enough trouble
> of its own. (Matthew 6:34).

Listening for His still small voice, I heard the word *counterstrike.* Chemotherapy is the counterstrike for the assault of cancer. It assaulted *me*, now *I* am fighting back! This revelation infused hope into my spirit as I no longer considered chemotherapy part of the problem, but the beginning of the solution. I had been bombarded with such a lengthy list of horrendous side effects that the very notion that it might save my life completely eluded me. The life preserver had walloped me so hard on the head that I almost forgot to hold on!

I spent the rest of the morning praising the Lord, desiring to be so immersed in His presence that I could handle anything. His peace enveloped me as I drew near to the one who loves me. With less than an hour to go before Lesley would pick me up, I sat quietly, meditating on the power of His cross. I felt it was important to take communion prior to every round of chemotherapy, as it would give me the opportunity to affirm my devotion to Jesus and to focus on His mighty power. Satan was defeated at the cross, and there was no better time to be reminded of that victory than before stepping out onto the battlefield. As I knelt down, bowing forward, my necklace fell towards my chin. The dangling cross was not just a piece of jewellery; it formed part of my arsenal. I had resolved to wear it until all my treatments were complete—a reminder of the covering that protects me.

In the few words that Jesus spoke from Calvary's cross, so much was revealed.

> It is finished (John 19:30).

Yes, every sickness, disease, and sin, including death itself has a place at the foot of the cross. In John 16:33 He says:

> In this world you will have trouble. But take heart! I
> have overcome the world.

As a child, I never understood why people wore crosses—a symbol of a horrible, torturous death. Now I see it as the embodiment of the highest form of love the world has ever known; the place where Jesus died for me. I love His cross and all it represents. As I closed my eyes I could see myself sitting beneath it, feeling the rough wood on my face as I wrapped both arms around it, holding on with all my strength. Hurricane winds seemed to rage around me as every truth of His word bubbled up from within. By faith I was clinging to every promise ever deposited in my heart, with hope giving me a reason to carry on.

The phone rang; it was time to leave. I slung my hospital goodie bag over my shoulder and locked the door behind me, knowing that in a few short hours I would be back, having conquered round one. Walking down the hall towards the elevator, I contemplated the verses I received a few moments before:

> Finally, be strong in the Lord and in his mighty power (Ephesians 6:10).

> They have not gained the victory over me (Psalm 129:2).

I had every hope in my commander. He had gone ahead of me, and He would never lead me into battle unprepared.

Upon arrival at the hospital, we took a quick tour of the sixth floor, getting acquainted with the chemo rooms, the jigsaw puzzle in the waiting area, and the selection of drinks and snacks available for those feeling queasy. The cancer agency runs a tight ship, keeping all scheduled appointment times, so with little delay we were met by a nurse who led us to her office. A long counter served as her desk and large cupboards overflowed with supplies. A private bathroom filled one corner. Four rather large reclining leather chairs were evenly spaced around the room, each with a visitor's chair off to one side. I made my way to one in front of a large picture window with a beautiful view of the city. This would give me something to focus on other than intravenous bags and needles.

I quickly learned that on every visit, whether the nurses were taking blood or administering drugs, they diligently verified my identity by asking my birth date. After reciting the month, day, and year as though it was my name, rank, and serial number, I light-heartedly pointed out that they were now expected to send me a birthday card. (I haven't received any cards yet—maybe next year.)

On this first visit, the nurse opened a large plastic bag full of massive vials containing three different drugs. I tried to remain calm as I watched it all unfold, still struggling to accept that this was really happening to me. Digging into my bag, I pulled out all the medications that my oncologist had prescribed for me. The nurse directed me to take some tablets before we started to avoid becoming nauseous. As everything was so new and unfamiliar, the whole process seemed to move very quickly. She wrapped my left arm in a large hot towel, readying the veins, while on my right side she fiddled with the intravenous stand. Needles, antiseptic, and sticky tape appeared on the small tray off the side of my armrest. A pillow was awkwardly placed behind the small of my back, and a heating pad rested on my other arm. I seemed to be in the midst of cords and tubes, unable to dart for the front door even if I tried.

I thought I would be hooked up to some kind of intravenous (IV) device and then left for a few hours while it drained into me, so I had brought some music to listen to, hoping that I could drift off to sleep and avoid the entire procedure. Much to my chagrin, this was not the case. The nurse sat herself in a chair at my left and handed me numerous papers, each listing the side effects for the different drugs. While working the needle into a vein, she went over the side effects, but her most immediate concern was that she had in fact *found* a vein so my flesh would not burn. When asked, I found it difficult to differentiate between the pain from the needle and the possibility that the drug was singeing my flesh. I could feel my blood pressure steadily rise as I waited for my hand to change colour. It didn't, so I guessed everything was okay. She steadily pushed each vial in through a vein in my hand and for more than an hour spoke fiery darts of doom, listing all the hazards. I was relieved to see the final bag placed on the

IV stand, which meant that she would wheel her chair back to her desk and away from me. As I laid my head against the back of the chair, I realized that my shoulders were so tense they were up around my ears. I had been so overwhelmed by what was going on that I had not even taken the time to recline the chair and get comfortable.

As I caught my breath, a woman in the chair next to me looked over and said,

"The first time is the worst."

The poison arrows continued to fly as she explained her first experience in the chemo chair. With no words of comfort mixed in with the poison, I became weary. I rolled my head to one side, choosing to look beyond the reality of my chair and focussing instead on the world beyond the walls. The sun was shining and life was carrying on out in the city. I looked up into the cloudless sky to see a large bird circling. As it drew nearer I could see that it was an eagle, and when it flew right past my window I knew that the Lord had just winked in my direction. His peace returned to me with this gentle reminder that He is still on His throne caring for His children.

A couple of hours later I was happy to be on my way home. Surprisingly, I was able to eat some dinner and, although I was feeling drugged up, I did not experience any nausea. Lesley stayed with me that first night in case I needed help; however I think I got more sleep than she did!

The next morning we were both relieved to see that I was doing well, particularly as the first twenty-four hours are usually the worst. At my insistence Lesley reluctantly went home to get some sleep. I carried on with the regime of prescriptions and slept on and off throughout the day.

For two days I nervously waited for the predicted side effects to manifest themselves. On the morning of the second day I was reminded of this verse:

> And these signs will accompany those who believe: In
> my name they will drive out demons; they will speak
> in new tongues; they will pick up snakes with their

hands; and **when they drink deadly poison, it will
not hurt them at all;** they will place their hands on
sick people, and they will get well (Mark 16:17—18.
Emphasis added).

Was I living proof of this scripture? I had just had poison injected into
my body and so far I had experienced no ill effects from it.

On the day prior to my first treatment the oncologist had
recommended a different protocol than what we had previously
discussed. She referred to it as a hotter mix, which immediately
brought to mind the promise in Isaiah:

But now, this is what the LORD says—he who created
you, O Jacob, he who formed you, O Israel: "Fear not,
for I have redeemed you; I have summoned you by
name; you are mine. When you pass through the
waters, I will be with you; and when you pass through
the rivers, they will not sweep over you. **When you
walk through the fire, you will not be burned; the
flames will not set you ablaze.** For I am the LORD,
your God, the Holy One of Israel, your Savior." (Isaiah
43:1–3. Emphasis added).

Although a hotter mix may not have been a welcome change, it meant
my treatments would be reduced to six from the original eight. I
was literally experiencing the living word of God as I saw Him work
miracles in and through me—a reduced treatment time and negligible
side effects in these first few critical days. These positive results were
far beyond my expectations.

*Lord, sustain the vision of what's beyond this fire. Keep
my eyes upon the goal, not the challenge—to see the
promise of your glory, not today's battles. Hide me in
the cleft of your rock so I might have your perfect peace
in the midst of this storm.*

This was the prayer I uttered during the first week as the time of grace appeared to end and my body succumbed to the effects of the drugs.

My stomach was the first to show signs of defeat, becoming extremely sensitive. My ever-changing appetite made it challenging to satisfy, as one minute I could eat fruit and a few moments later the very thought of it made me nauseous. For five days I suffered from bouts of diarrhea that nearly killed me as I quickly became dehydrated with periods of light-headedness that frightened me. Having rarely required prescriptions or over-the-counter medications, my ignorance led me to believe that one standard dose of those drugs would cure me. As the days rolled on I steadily increased the dosage, finally realizing that I needed to respond more aggressively to my situation—lightweight solutions were out of the question as I was battling a giant. This was a real wakeup call to me as, having rejected my body for so many years I was forming a new relationship with it and taking up the responsibility to fight for its health. In one day I used more medications than I had in ten years.

Unable to stand for more than five minutes at a time, I put in a food emergency call to my friend Kathy, who showed up on my doorstep armed with white bread and white rice. Within a few hours I began to gain strength, grateful to have found a solution. Nightfall had come and one more day was marked off the calendar.

Sunday came and I forced myself to go to church, knowing I would receive a much-needed jolt of strength from the Lord. I was blessed to receive prayers that were not simply for healing, but powerful proclamations of God's promises that breathed new life into my spirit. In these first few weeks, the enemy was steadily trying to undermine my faith and blur my vision. The circumstances in the natural (my body) were beginning to overwhelm the strength I had in my spirit, so I was gradually losing sight of my future and all the good things that it held. I had never experienced an assault of this magnitude in my life, and predictably, it came with a lesson from the Lord on how to combat it.

In the weeks to come, He showed me how our body is an integral part of our spiritual defence. If we are sick, we simply cannot function effectively. If the enemy can destroy the temple, our body, we have nowhere to reside. He also taught me how to fight when physically I had nothing left to give. It is one thing to fight when you are full of natural energy, but quite another when you are horizontal and struggling for the privilege to take another breath.

Two weeks after the first treatment, my hair started to fall out—right on schedule. I thought it would be brittle and break off in various lengths but instead, it just fell out as though the roots did not have the strength or will to hold on to the strands. My good friend, Tracy, owned a proper salon razor and was expecting my call. Together we agreed that Sunday would be razor day.

(Previously during a visit to their home the Lord had used her husband Mike to prepare me for losing my hair. Mike had agreed to let his eight-year-old nephew give him a haircut. A couple of hours later he walked through the front door with a trim that was laughable. The young boy wanted to cut Uncle Mike's hair with no guard on the razor, so a couple of unwanted bald patches adorned one side of his head. To fix things, Tracy had to shave his entire head so the cut would be even. Mike handled the situation with such grace and humour that it spoke volumes to me. I realized that it was just hair, and as the doctor had clearly said, "It *always* grows back." Only later did I realize how much I needed to hear those words.)

Tracy has always been someone who gets right down to the task at hand, and so I knew there would be no discussion and that procrastination was not an option. I placed a stool in the middle of the kitchen floor, far from any mirror. She arrived and in an effort to minimize the awkwardness of this moment went briskly to work. Choosing to shave in style, I played an upbeat Motown song loud enough to drown out the daunting hum of the razor. Within minutes she was done and I was completely bald. Although it was all business, Tracy's heart of compassion could not be hidden as she sent me off to the shower while she swept the floor, so I would not have to look at the damage.

Standing beneath the comforting warmth of the shower, I

welcomed the quiet moments I had to myself as I grasped what had just occurred. I was alone with my thoughts, which would reveal the truth of my response. In the weeks leading up to this hurdle I was preparing for an onslaught of tears. Instead I was consumed with relief that this day had finally arrived and I had overcome its challenges.

chapter nine

A Cast of Thousands

The Lord is my banner.
EXODUS 17:15

A pamphlet in the information folder from the surgeon contained a pullout navigational map for patients and families, depicting a girl riding a bicycle along the breast cancer treatment path, beginning with the diagnosis and ending with post treatment follow-up. It included timelines and strategic points along the way for decisions.

In the days leading up to my first chemo session, the Lord sketched His *own* roadmap for me. His love painted the background of the page, and the road signs of decisions were supported by Godly wisdom and revelation. Angels accompanied me and the cross was always before me. Along the way He gave me courage by causing me to face my fears, and faith that served as fuel to keep pace. The road called Hope went far beyond where the eye could see into a bright horizon of an exciting future. The Lord went ahead of me to forge the path and although visibility may have been limited, I always had enough light to see where to take my next step. As I continued to move forward, I could see marquees of promises up ahead. Hope and excitement flooded my heart about all the Lord had called me to do and all that He had yet to accomplish.

As the groundwork was laid for *His* plans, He also pointed out potholes and clouds where the enemy was hiding. Discouragement and loneliness were constant adversaries to my hope and faith.

In Luke 22, we read how Simon's faith was tested.

> Simon, Simon, Satan has asked to sift you as wheat. But I have prayed for you, Simon, that your faith may not fail (vv.31—32).

The Lord knew what Simon would do, but *Simon* needed the lesson. (It is interesting that the Lord addressed him by his old name "Simon," not "Peter"—an indication that the *old* nature of Simon with all of his ungodly instincts was being revealed.) When he realized that the Lord had correctly predicted that three times he would deny knowing Jesus, it shattered him but brought him to humility and repentance.

I began to see that the substance of our convictions is tested when there is still an opportunity for change. When we have a crisis of faith, the enemy plans to leave us spiritually bankrupt. The Lord however, uses it to expose our heart so in humility we can draw near to find the righteousness of God, honing our character into His likeness.

At times the Lord allowed me to be cloistered away from all outside influence, yet He often brought faithful servants He calls friends to be His hands and feet. Cancer does not just affect the victims; it touches the lives of everyone around them. Friends and family were such an essential part of my roadmap as I benefited from an entire support network working under a banner called love. Cheering me on, their kindness nurtured in me the will to continue, with a hope to emerge victorious.

I am compelled to include this chapter in recognition of those who so willingly helped me and whose love watered my seeds of faith and displayed the very heart of Jesus. My hope is that it will be an encouragement to those who are walking with a loved one who has been diagnosed with cancer. For the patient, my prayer is that it will release you to say "yes" to those offering to carry the burden with you.

Being an independent person, I knew I would be challenged to ask for help. I had already been smothered by wellwishers offering advice, so great discernment was a necessity in balancing my needs with the willingness of those around me who were anxious to help. I wanted to be sensitive to others, particularly close family and friends, knowing that their catharsis was to physically *do* something. Many people have a heart to help cancer victims whether it is simply opening a door or participating in walks or marathons to raise money for cancer research. This experience gave me more of a heart for the general population as I was blessed by the selfless kindness of strangers on many occasions.

We only have to turn on the evening news to see the sad state of our world, so it is heartening to see people come to the aid of those in need. We can easily lose faith in humanity until tragedy strikes in our own backyard. It is then that the true heroes arise.

In the aftermath of the tsunami that struck Thailand, Indonesia, Sri Lanka, and other South Asian countries in December 2004, it was the personal stories that touched me the most—men, women, and children who through sacrificial giving and prayer brought life and hope back to villages that had been decimated.

A few years earlier the tragedy of 9/11 brought countless expressions of love and compassion from all over the world. Again, it was the personal testimonies of divine and human intervention that were so touching for many of us. In the comfort and safety of my living room I watched in horror as the second plane hit the World Trade Centre—an unbelievable tragic drama unfolding on national television. I wept for the victims and their families, all the while feeling helpless at not being able to do anything. However, sadness and grief over the unnecessary loss of lives and the injustice of terrorism provided the catalyst to stir me to action, and so I fasted and prayed throughout the day for the individuals, the cities, and the entire nation. As I cried out to the Lord, I felt His comfort for my grieving heart and the reassurance that this same mercy and grace were indeed being poured out upon a nation in turmoil.

Hearing the word "cancer" can evoke varying emotions, from

denial to an assumption of death. It may not be a catastrophic world event, but it feels like a tsunami to those directly affected. As the bearer of bad news, I found it a daunting task to tell others of my situation as I felt completely ill-equipped to deal with their response and questions. I started taking on their burdens since I was the one that had upset them. It was not long before my countenance began to reveal signs of weariness from carrying this excess baggage.

> Come to me, all you who are weary and burdened,
> and I will give you rest (Matthew 11:28).

The Lord gently reminded me that He was more than able to care for their troubled hearts *and* carry my load.

After depositing my burdens at the cross, once again I asked for God's direction as I embarked upon a journey that clearly required an entire crew. I laid down my pride (as much as would willingly go), asking the Lord to give me humility to ask for help, and wisdom to choose the right people. Instead of sailing solo, my team was soon hopping aboard.

Lesley was such a blessing when she accompanied me at the beginning and throughout the process of discovery. I felt no apprehension in sharing the most intimate details of my treatment with her and I appreciated having someone to talk to. She did her best to keep a brave face through every appointment, while I knew she was crying inside. Some of the most precious times with her were when she would walk through my front door and I would run to embrace my big sister as I burst into tears. My stoic cover was blown, yet my transparency brought a deep richness to our relationship.

Many asked how they could assist me and to their great disappointment, I was unable to give them tangible answers as I did not know how each round of chemotherapy would go or how I would feel, so I did not *know* what I needed! To my great delight, some very creative friends took the initiative to come up with ideas that were just perfect. I credit the Lord with whispering in their ear as these surprises always arrived at just the right time.

Many offered helpful books on breast cancer and other subjects such as nutrition, survivor testimonies, interesting autobiographies, and easy-reading, light-hearted novels. I received healthy recipes and bags of groceries of thoughtfully selected items. A juicer was donated to the cause after I discovered the benefits of freshly squeezed fruit juice. Others, sympathetic to my bouts of nausea, sent chocolate for those days when I just did not care about the calories, and ice cream to help me through the long hot days of summer. Flowers would sporadically arrive, giving me something refreshingly different to stare at from my sofa and serving as a simple reminder that I was loved. I received lovely scarves and hand-picked gifts with heartfelt messages that blessed and encouraged me. Music CDs were a great blessing and a welcome change from my own collection. One friend was so generous as to buy me an MP3 player and load it up with uplifting worship songs, knowing that I had no strength to do it myself. Another was inspired by my journey to write a touching worship song. Elizabeth, the friend I mentioned earlier, was a great support in my early stages and continued to check in with me. An accomplished pianist, she went to the trouble of borrowing a karaoke machine and recording forty-five minutes of beautiful praise music, which arrived on a day I when I was feeling blue. My prayer had been "Lord, bring encouragement today," and in His faithfulness this gift dropped through my mail slot. She later confessed the blessing she had experienced while recording it.

Another friend gave me a cross necklace that had belonged to her mother. I know what it meant for her to give this away, as for thirty-three years it had brought her comfort through every trial she had endured. Her deep expression of love and compassion was not just words, but a true sacrifice.

Before my surgery, a lady and her daughter had thoughtfully made a beautiful plaque for me with a poem reminding me of all the wonderful things that cancer *cannot* take away, including friendships and love. How appropriate that it was one of the first gifts I received, and over the course of nine months I learned that every line of it was true. I treasured the heart of each individual that made time in their day for me and who made an extra effort to bless me in their own unique way with gifts that the Lord had given them.

I was truly humbled to see the hands of the Lord at work through every act of kindness from family and friends: in every ride that was offered, every outing, every phone call (some even calling long distance while on vacation), email, and card. One dear friend faithfully sent cards every couple of weeks—most intended to make me laugh; others with a cheery note, a prayer, or an encouraging word.

One of the greatest demonstrations of love was the outpouring of prayer that came from my church family, who presented countless prayers before the throne of grace in heaven on my behalf at all hours of the day and night.

> Let us then approach the throne of grace with confidence, so that we may receive mercy and find grace to help us in our time of need (Hebrews 4:16).

Intercessors were diligent to ask about my specific needs so that they could pray with accuracy and precision to bring healing and comfort from the hand of God. A pastor from another church was also faithful to pray with his congregation on my behalf; indicative of the true body of Christ that has no denominational boundaries. I believe in the power of fervent prayer and thank the Lord for providing so many who selflessly fell to their knees for me.

In the kingdom of God, there is an irrevocable law that says we reap what we sow.

> Remember this: Whoever sows sparingly will also reap sparingly, and whoever sows generously will also reap generously (2 Corinthians 9:6).

When confiding my complete surprise at the extent of support, one precious saint reminded me of all the prayers I had uttered for others. Now I was seeing the fruit of my labour returning as a blessing in my hour of need. Similarly, I saw the promise of God fulfilled to care for my every need in the area of finances. In the well-known Psalm 23, David writes of the Lord's provision.

The Lord is my Shepherd, I shall not be in want (v.1).

Mixed in amongst all the concerns about my health was the reality that I no longer had an income. I did not have extended medical coverage, and the government's fifteen-week payment plan would not begin to pay the bills. My only hope was that my savings account would not run dry. Before I was faced with dipping into my savings, my parents generously offered to provide for me financially throughout my treatment. This was such an unexpected blessing as I had witnessed their life of dedicated hard work, stretching every dollar to get the most out of it. As immigrants from the United Kingdom, they had arrived in Canada shortly after World War II with little in their pocket. Since then, they had made many sacrifices to provide for our family, never spending money frivolously (they rarely travel or eat out). This benevolent gesture completely freed me from any looming financial burden, affording me the comfort and convenience of staying in my own apartment which was home.

> "Bring the whole tithe into the storehouse, that there may be food in my house. Test me in this," says the LORD Almighty, "and see if I will not throw open the floodgates of heaven and pour out so much blessing that you will not have room enough for it" (Malachi 3:10).

I have faithfully tithed on all that the Lord has placed in my hands as well as given generously to ministries, outreaches, and individuals. I also funded all my mission trips, leaving generous gifts behind in the nations I was privileged to serve. At times I saw my bank account dwindle and questioned when I would see a return on my investment. *Perhaps this will be the treasure I am storing up in heaven*, I would reassure myself. This gesture from my parents served as a humbling reminder that the Lord has ways that are so much higher than my ways. Never could I have imagined that a portion of my return would come in one lump sum, but He was faithful to me once again.

As I reflect on His provision, I see how many pairs of hands He has used to bring His blessings. This cast of thousands, was His army who willingly offered to serve with no compensation. As they walked through adversity with me, I felt that lost relationships had been restored and existing ones strengthened. I emerged with many friends, both old and new, whom I hold dear in my heart.

In the book of Exodus, Joshua led the fight against the Amalekites while Moses, Aaron and Hur climbed a hill to watch his victory.

> As long as Moses held up his hands, the Israelites were winning, but whenever he lowered his hands, the Amalekites were winning. When Moses' hands grew tired, they took a stone and put it under him and he sat on it. Aaron and Hur held his hands up— one on one side, one on the other—so that his hands remained steady till sunset (Exodus 17:11–12).

Just as Aaron and Hur lifted Moses arms when he had become weary, I had troops strengthening my arms throughout this battle. Their collective efforts not only assured the victory, but continually reaffirmed my faith that God's watchful eye is always upon His people. With a grateful heart I declare that the Lord is my banner and I will proclaim this truth to the nations.

> For great is your love, higher than the heavens; your faithfulness reaches to the skies Be exalted, O God, above the heavens, and let your glory be over all the earth. (Psalm 108:4–5).

chapter ten

Healing in His Wings

For you who revere my name, the sun of
righteousness will rise with healing in its wings.
MALACHI 4:2

"BLAST OFF!" The space shuttle had launched for another journey into space—finally something interesting to turn my attention to on TV during these long days of solitude on the sofa. I giggled with great excitement as I watched the lift off—no more delays, it was finally taking off. It is exhilarating to see the rocket boosters fire up, listen to the countdown, see the crowd holding their breath, and await the movement of such a massive machine as it starts its journey into another realm. The space shuttle project is such a fitting example of an entire team working towards a common goal. A handful of astronauts share the spotlight before lift-off, but thousands of other people work for countless hours to ensure the mission's success. There are so many more days of preparation than that of the actual trip in space. In some ways this reminds me of the preparation of God's people who, down through the ages, have carried the baton in establishing the kingdom of God—each generation waiting with eager anticipation for the Lord's return.

As a child I was taught the Lord's Prayer and remember the words "your kingdom come, your will be done on earth as it is in heaven"

(Matthew 6:10). Reflecting upon it now, I am certain that I recited it more as a poem by rote rather than with an understanding of its meaning. I had an "aha" moment when, as an adult, I realized I had a part in ushering in His kingdom and preparing for His return! If I really expect His kingdom to come, then my responsibility is to be an expression of His Godly character. His goodness, kindness, gentleness, patience, joy, peace, faithfulness, self-control, and love can be established through anyone who offers to be a willing vessel—but such valuable qualities do not evolve without great sacrifice.

With a sincere desire to be used of the Lord to bless others, I confessed my willingness to do anything and go anywhere. I often became puzzled when my life did not look the way I thought it should, and my seasons of preparation seemed to be never-ending. Every time I took inventory, I was back in His refining fire again, with the heat being turned up a notch.

Lord, I know I need training, but when can I go?
My patience and hope were tested whenever I would see friends commissioned as missionaries and sent forth to the nations. Countless reports would reach us detailing the abundance of transformed souls, and villages that were touched through the work of these individuals. I so longed to be among those making a difference, but it seemed that my time had not yet come. Had I missed the call? Did someone forget to send me the memo?

Working on the mission field is a great privilege and gratifying when the locals shower you with appreciation. Nothing is more rewarding than putting food in the belly of a starving child or building a home for a family that sleeps on the dirt beneath a roof made of cardboard. However, if we are motivated by self- gratification, our testimony of Jesus' love will be short lived.

Surprisingly, some of my greatest lessons on the mission field were not about coping with culture shock or the challenges of living in a developing nation, but rather in fostering grace when dealing with team dynamics. Mixing numerous take charge personalities in a confined space can only be a God-appointed training field for personal sacrifice. Most people can put on a good face in normal circumstances, but masks often crack under pressure. Strife inevitably reveals all its partners in crime including the desire to be in control and ultimately, our pride. Ouch!

In order to produce good fruit in keeping with the qualities of Christ, we must endure the seasons of planting and pruning. As new buds begin to form, the very nature of Christ's love begins to bloom. This love is not just *acts* of kindness or words of comfort and prayer, but a genuine force that conquers all. It is the motivation for all that we put our hand to and the source of power behind our enduring strength. Though not easily acquired, this characteristic is a precious gem deeply buried within the very heart of God that is available to those who passionately seek Him.

God does not do anything haphazardly, but rather with methodical, careful planning. There is an appointed time for everything and when we are patient we will see His perfect plan unfold in a way that is nothing short of brilliant.

> For the revelation awaits an appointed time; it speaks
> of the end and will not prove false. Though it linger,
> wait for it; it will certainly come and will not delay
> (Habakkuk 2:3).

For every challenge I have faced, the Lord has taught me to stop blaming others and check my own heart first. Regardless of where the fault lies, I need to be able to respond with righteousness, forgiveness, and love. When things are not done our way, the enemy sneaks in to bring division, leading us to defeat. Much of the preparation the Lord does within us is to remove our habit of selfishness and replace it with His perfect love that seeks every opportunity to serve. Our actions do not need to be seen by anyone when we purpose in our heart to honour the Lord. It is our love for Him that sets us free from the bondage of satisfying our own desires. These instincts go deep, but similarly, so does His love. When we begin to tap into this source, the results are amazing as we find grace for those who hurt us, and hearts become transformed. The Lord is not moved so much by our words but by our sacrifices. As our eyes are focused on Him instead of ourselves, we begin to reflect His glorious countenance. Some of the highest callings require the greatest preparation.

More of you, Lord; less of me

Over the next few months as my body became weaker, I experienced the Lord digging down into remote places to tear out the old roots of hidden sins. Some of these detrimental footholds stemmed back to previous generations, with consequences that still influenced my life. With every new round of revelation and repentance my hope rested in the belief that my sinful character would be replaced by the fullness of who He is.

Sofa time was abundant throughout my treatment, leading to great times of reflection. In the depth of my valleys I even questioned my calling. *Would I be sent out to the ends of the earth? Would He use my hands to heal the sick? Could I be one that delivers this message of life? Will I ever be ready?* The Lord was allowing such a shaking to occur that it rattled my very foundations.

> Ask of me, and I will make the nations your inheritance,
> the ends of the earth your possession (Psalm 2:8).

Many, many times I would cry out to the Lord for the nations—I would weep for the lost souls who were scattered in the far corners of the world. With a sense of purpose and passion, I felt a small portion of His monumental burden for the nations that did not yet know Him as a Father who loves them.

However, as time marched on, I began to wonder if my own desires had clouded my calling from on high. I needed to find the courage to ask myself if I truly had a heart for the nations, sensing that the response would set the course for the rest of my life.

> Now faith is being sure of what we hope for and certain
> of what we do not see (Hebrews 11:1).

As the Lord tested my faith, I also needed to be certain of what I was hoping for. How could I run a race with perseverance if I did not know what track I was on? He was answering my prayer for clear vision and to have ears to hear the clarion call upon my life. As He developed His heart of love within me, I covenanted to be committed for the long haul until my assignment was completed—the first job application I would complete with certainty of purpose and a commitment to stay the course.

Over the span of a career, it is rare to find anyone who has remained with one company, earning the coveted traditional gold watch at retirement. Our generation has discovered the freedom to make our own decisions, do what we want to, and move on to something else if we get bored or simply do not like our boss. Conversely, employers rarely make a long-term commitment to individuals, favouring whatever hiring methods that satisfy a more profitable bottom line instead of fostering an environment of mutual loyalty. Although our democratic society has given us precious freedom, it has also encouraged a mindset of independence and self-reliance.

A kingdom mindset however, is more gold-watch-oriented with a long-term commitment and is dependant upon complete trust in the King and His goodness and decree for us. Each of us has one calling that has been perfectly planned from the foundation of the earth and is not to be taken lightly. We trust that He has our best interests at heart and is fully invested in seeing us succeed—He is completely, 100 percent committed to us in every way.

During this time of contemplation on kingdom business, my mind was so preoccupied with thoughts about my calling that I tended to be withdrawn when in a crowd. One Monday evening I attended a prayer meeting and quietly took my place a few rows back from the altar. As we rose to our feet to start our time of praise, I closed my eyes, dropped my head, and began to focus on the Lord. With no time to guard my response, a song based on Psalm 2:8 rang through the speakers and directly into my heart…*"the nations as your inheritance"*.

Could this be for me? I fell to my knees and wept as I realized the

Lord was repeating back to me the very desire of my heart. He was breathing new life into the tarnished promise I had tossed into the questionable pile. We began to pray with fervency for the multitudes around the world and my tears of sorrow for the lost were mixed with ones of joy as I experienced a revival of purpose. My love for His nations returned with an overwhelming passion.

That night I felt like I had met with the King. He confirmed my calling in the most unusual way by overpowering me with His love as though I was swirling in a smooth and warm river of oil moving with purpose around me. The hope of my calling was nourished and strengthened as His heart for the nations continued to pour over me. I was intoxicated by His love and passion as every sense was stirred by His fragrance. This small sampling of heaven was exquisite, leaving me hungry for more. What a challenge it must be for Him to come down to our level and contain the depth of His richness when He wants to unleash the fullness of His kingdom upon us. An earthly canvas can hardly portray the infinite beauty of our Lord.

As I was gaining strength in preparation for my next round of chemo, the Lord was healing old wounds as He re-established His calling for me. This theme carried on into the morning when I again took communion before heading to the clinic. My practice was to sit in silence, knowing He would whisper a word of truth into my spirit.

> But for you who revere my name, the sun of righteousness will rise with healing in its wings. And you will go out and leap like calves released from the stall (Malachi 4:2).

> Then your light will break forth like the dawn, and your healing will quickly appear; then your righteousness will go before you, and the glory of the LORD will be your rear guard (Isaiah 58:8).

I was comforted by the assurance that He was healing every part of me in preparation for a greater purpose.

I longed to linger in His presence, but was aware of the deadline to leave for the hospital. Choosing to walk in the truth that my healing was imminent, I selected a pink shirt that day, as pink often represents healing. Opening the car door I smiled and hugged my friend who, for no apparent reason, had also decided to wear pink as she escorted me downtown for my treatment. Later I recalled that friends often referred to her as "Pinky." God is so quick to confirm His closeness through even the smallest details. Every attempt of the enemy to sow seeds of doubt was quickly thwarted by the powerful blows of God's commanding presence.

Walking into the cancer agency, I noticed that the anxieties of my previous visits had been squashed. I was now familiar with the surroundings and the procedure itself, which strengthened my confidence as I made my way to the sixth floor. I found my chair by the window and reclined to a comfortable position, ready for the injections. The atmosphere had changed as I felt that the Lord had already prepared the way, and His presence accompanied me. No fiery darts of predicted side effects, but instead a conversation with the nurse that led to a discussion about the Bible. We talked about the life of the apostle Paul, who endured great suffering. It was interesting to parallel the events from biblical times to lives of present-day saints. One thing that remains unchanged is that we all experience trials.

Looking around the room, I felt completely alert to all that was happening, unlike the first visit when my fear was almost tangible. A woman directly across from me, who was hooked up to an IV device, was struggling with a persistent cough, her lungs so irritated that every breath seemed to be a challenge. For more than an hour she suffered with it, apologizing for the disruption to those around her. It suddenly occurred to me to quietly pray for healing. Within moments the coughing ceased and a peace enveloped her. What power can be released through one heartfelt prayer! Even *she* seemed surprised that the coughing stopped.

To my left was a woman who started sharing the details of her pending operation and seemed fearful about what lay ahead. Attributing all her strength to be found from within, she believed that her personal "energy line" would be cut by the surgery on her chest, depleting her supply. She offered to meet with me to discuss alternative medicines that she believed in, but I politely declined her offer and confessed my faith in the power of Jesus. Not sure how to respond, she smiled and went back to her magazine as I silently lifted her up in prayer, asking the Lord to give her the same hope He had given me. My prayers had a deeper sincerity born out of a true compassion for the lost. I saw her through His eyes with a heart of love, not judgment; with sadness that she did not know the One who loves her and longs to be her source of strength.

As the Lord dealt with my fears, a boldness to speak the truth in love accompanied the shift that occurred.

> For God did not give us a spirit of timidity, but a spirit of power, of love and of self-discipline (2 Timothy 1:7).

This time I was not on the defence, but on the *offence*, ready to snatch one from the fire and give them life.

> Perfect love casts out fear (1 John 4:18 NKJV®).

Having experienced His perfect love, I was no longer fearful. In fact, my hope had been renewed as the God of all comfort flooded me with His glory.

That morning when we arrived, the parking lot had been full, forcing us to park on the open-air roof. Stealing a few moments to enjoy the warmth of the sun on my face, I tilted my head back and looked up into the clear blue sky, delighted to see "my" eagle again circling directly overhead.

> He gives strength to the weary and increases the power of the weak. Even youths grow tired and weary, and young men stumble and fall; but those who hope in the LORD will renew their strength. They will soar on

wings like eagles; they will run and not grow weary,
they will walk and not be faint. (Isaiah 40:29–31).

Although I was not yet ready to fly, I was confident in the transformation that was happening to mature this little eaglet. Only after my wounded soul was healed, my broken body restored, and my spirit lifted could I fly with strength and endurance. He was tuning my vision to be as sharp as the eagle's, able to remain focused on the purpose and destination even at great distances. Upon His command I would hear the countdown to be tossed from the nest, ready to spread my wings and soar to new heights.

chapter eleven

Weary Warrior

Surely he will save you from the fowler's
snare and from the deadly pestilence.
PSALM 91:3

With surgery and a couple of treatments behind me, I was now beginning to understand more about the battle at hand. Each new lesson was a great encouragement knowing that every small victory was one step closer to the ultimate triumph: breast cancer would be defeated.

God's hand was evident on every side and my trust and confidence in Him continued to grow as I heard the voice and leading of my commander. When I longed for a rest from the battle, He made it clear that a time-out was not an option and that any hesitation on my part would result in losing ground. I needed to remain alert and vigilant, knowing that the enemy was right on my heels. I have often heard the expression that "we pick our battles." Although this one was not my choice, I could not ignore it as denial would have meant certain death. I am sure that many soldiers are fighting a war that is not theirs, hoping for a time when peace will reign. But does that possibility even exist?

Dating back to the Garden of Eden at the fall of man, strife has existed in the world. In Genesis chapter four we read about two brothers, Cain and Abel, whose rivalry resulted in the death of Abel. As time went on and sin ran rampant, the Lord became so grieved by the earth that He flooded it only six chapters after He created it! The very nature of sin is the makings of war and unrest.

> But if you do not do what is right, sin is crouching at your door; it desires to have you, but you must master it" (Genesis 4:7).

What remains today is the battle of sin within us and between one another. We are caught in the crossfire of light colliding with darkness; good fighting for its place over evil.

Throughout the Old Testament we find numerous accounts of great battles that paint a shocking portrait of sin's consequences, so fierce that it has set nation against nation. As we move into the New Testament letters, the apostle Paul reminds us of the spiritual battle we are in:

> For our struggle is . . . against the spiritual forces of evil in the heavenly realms (Ephesians 6:12).

The good news is that the battle belongs to the Lord and great blessings are bestowed upon those who obediently follow after Him.

> You will be blessed in the city and blessed in the country. You will be blessed when you come in and blessed when you go out. The LORD will send a blessing on your barns and on everything you put your hand to. The LORD your God will bless you in the land he is giving you. The LORD will open the heavens, the storehouse of his bounty, to send rain on your land in season and to bless all the work of your hands (Deuteronomy 28:3, 6, 8, 12).

Blessings, blessings and even *more* blessings. So, on the battlefield called cancer, drowning in a pool of my own tears, my heart asked, *Where are these promised blessings?* With a deafening silence from heaven, I began to see that my answers do not always lie in the depth of today's valley, but beyond the horizon of tomorrow. With every slash of the sword, I must press on, choosing to trust and believe.

While contemplating the reality of war, I thought back to a recent trip to England when I had the opportunity to view the fascinating display of arms and armour in the Tower of London. Enormous suits of all shapes and sizes for men (and their horses!) stood tall above the onlookers, who strained to imagine the days of old. With my nose up against the glass showcase, I moved as close as possible to get the full impact of what I was seeing. How brave those warriors were as they galloped towards their enemy with a shield in one hand and sword in the other, face guards limiting their vision and the sheer weight of their armour reducing their mobility. Although these pieces were polished for display purposes, I could imagine the dents and scratches that told of tales of war. One area showcased the large, personal armour of Henry VIII, reminding me that even kings went to war.

Thankfully, in the spiritual battle we wage in North America today for the kingdom of God we seldom see much blood, although this is beginning to change. In many parts of the world there has been bloodshed for generations in the name of religion. With a wounded soul, we can still feel the effects in a number of ways. Our mind can be tormented to such an extent that we become confused and in extreme cases, find ourselves in a state of chaos. Similarly, when attacked by infirmity our bodies can be knocked down, rendering us completely useless. So how do we overcome these very real assaults?

"The gateway of our greatest agony is the gateway to our greatest victory." This revelation came to our pastor as our tour group stood in the garden of Gethsemane, looking across to the Eastern Gate of the Temple Mount in Jerusalem. It was in this garden that Jesus experienced such anguish, sweating blood on the eve of His crucifixion. Upon His triumphant return, the Bible tells us that He will establish His throne in Jerusalem—the place of His greatest agony. As battle fatigue hounded me, the Lord led me to play the DVD of my trip to Israel and hear these words of truth for what seemed like the first time.

The Lord then reminded me of another instance when I encountered this type of fatigue in a similar scenario—I was tired and weary with no end in sight. A few years ago I was asked to fill in as the leader of a prayer group one Saturday morning. After we finished up, one of the participants followed me out to the parking lot, engaging me in a hot debate. She vehemently disagreed with me on the subject of depression and verbally abused me. I was so shocked by her actions that I was unable to utter a single word. Something came over me that could only be explained as sheer exhaustion—as though the life had been sucked right out of me. My limbs felt like lead as I struggled to climb into my car.

By this time, the parking lot had emptied and I sat alone in my car. Completely spent, I was incapable of driving home. *How could this verbal assault carry so much weight?* Closing my eyes, every last bit of strength was poured into my cry for help from the Lord. Immediately, I was in a vision—a battlefield with both sides fully engaged in the fight. A flurry of activity ensued in every direction with clouds of gun smoke and soldiers on the move.

"Soldier down! Medic! Medic!" I heard.

I saw myself lying in the deep thick mud, struggling to remain conscious while listening to the faint sounds of warriors running around me continuing the fight. Somehow I had become encased in a bulletproof Plexiglas® bubble. Jesus was kneeling in the mud with my head in His lap as He gently comforted me. My sense was that nobody could see us, and that the medics had been dispatched on my behalf. This spiritual assault had taken me by surprise, as did the power it had to break my spirit. In my ignorance, I did not yet understand how God uses these situations to teach us and *strengthen* us. The exhaustion only led me to feel defeated, preferring to remain in the presence of the Lord forever instead of continuing the pilgrimage to find my purpose and destiny for my life on earth. Without speaking, the Lord knew my thoughts, and replied to my request to be taken home. He said,

It is not time yet.

Without words, we continued our dialogue, Spirit to spirit. Before that day, I had never experienced this deep level of peace, which only increased my desire to be taken home. Being in the all encompassing, loving presence of Jesus was so inviting, that I did not want to come back.

At the Lord's direction, I opened my eyes briefly and I was back in the present, sitting in my car in the empty lot. A young woman of about eighteen was standing just a few feet from my car, fussing over her dog and seemingly unaware of my presence. In my spirit, I heard the Lord's voice responding to my deep desire to stay with Him.

If you come home now, who will tell her about me?

The girl possessed an innocence that ignited grief and injustice within me over the possibility of her spending an eternity in hell. I closed my eyes again and returned to the overwhelming peace of the Lord's presence.

A few moments later, two vehicles entered the parking garage and to my surprise, chose to park on either side of *my* car in the midst of a completely empty lot. The eight to ten occupants also seemed unaware of my presence and jumped out of their vehicles and carried on an animated conversation with one another over my car. I again heard,

Who will tell them about me?

I returned to the vision and gradually felt my strength return. We hovered a while longer on the mud-strewn battlefield until the medics arrived. The vision ended as I put my key in the ignition.

Without delay, I mustered the strength to speak out a prayer of salvation for all the people the Lord had used in the parking lot to make His point. I uttered my commitment to finish the work assigned to me here on earth, knowing the Lord would always be with me. Throughout the short drive home I felt as if an ambulance was carrying me. Although I could see my hands on the steering wheel, I felt certain that someone else was driving. Softly praying, I concentrated on driving at the speed limit, even though it seemed as if I was traveling much faster. I dragged myself out of the car and up to my apartment, collapsing onto my bed. Four hours later I awoke with a fresh perspective on the intensity of this war.

Same battle, different battlefield

I knew that the enemy was trying to destroy me with this deadly disease called cancer. The victory would not be quick, but I knew the Lord would give me a strategy to overcome.

> Surely he will save you from the fowler's snare and from the deadly pestilence. He will cover you with his feathers, and under his wings you will find refuge; his faithfulness will be your shield and rampart. You will not fear the terror of night, nor the arrow that flies by day, nor the pestilence that stalks in the darkness, nor the plague that destroys at midday (Psalm 91:3—6).

Nobody can begin to understand why God chooses to miraculously heal some in a single moment and not others, but we hold onto the hope that something good will come of the experience.

> Not only so, but we also rejoice in our sufferings, because we know that suffering produces perseverance; perseverance, character; and character, hope. And hope does not disappoint us, because God has poured out his love into our hearts by the Holy Spirit, whom he has given us. (Romans 5:3-5).

Perseverance is not quickly acquired, but is the product of our ongoing belief and hopes for tomorrow.

Approaching my third round of chemo, I was given another key to freedom by way of *A More Excellent Way*™, a book by Henry W. Wright, who I had seen on television a few years previously. He believes there is a connection between sin and disease and recounted amazing stories of people with all sorts of ailments who were healed through very specific prayer. When we find the root cause of our illness, we can be set free through repentance in prayer.

During the interview, Wright had described two separate incidents where each woman suffered from breast cancer. One had a tumour in her right breast; the other a tumour in her left breast. As they prayed, the Lord revealed that bitterness was the root that needed prayerful consideration. One woman confessed a bitterness that had developed against her own child. The other woman discovered a root of bitterness towards her mother. Deeply convicted of their sin, they each prayed through forgiving those who had hurt them and repented for carrying bitterness. Each one experienced a miraculous healing as the tumours dissolved.

It is difficult to say if this is the definitive answer for each person diagnosed with breast cancer, but it rang true for me, and so I decided that there was nothing lost in simply asking the Lord to reveal the truth. As I waited in prayer, He convicted my heart as He reminded me of the bitterness I had displayed towards my mother when I was a teenager. It could have been classified as typical teen behaviour, but it did not negate the fact that we had had many disagreements that opened the door to strong resentments and frustrations. Mum and I had long since resolved our differences, but roots run deep and often go unnoticed.

Throughout numerous discussions with my family, we methodically pieced together incidents from the past. We realized that bitterness towards mothers existed on both sides of the family and could be traced back at least three generations. Interesting coincidence?

> See to it that no one misses the grace of God and that
> no bitter root grows up to cause trouble and defile
> many (Hebrews 12:15).

In prayer I interceded on behalf of all my ancestors that had bitter judgments against mothers, seeking God's forgiveness for them and for my part in this same sin. I believe the Lord lifted this curse off our family and me through my act of sincere repentance.

Our God is holy; He does not change. He is the same yesterday, today and forever so we must honour and respect His ordinances. Some may ask why a God of love can allow His children to become sick or even die prematurely. Others may question why it is our responsibility to make amends for the sins of our forefathers. The word of God says that people perish for lack of knowledge. The truth is available to us, but we have the responsibility to seek Him and find the answers. Some people choose to worship a god they have formed from their own desires, whom they think God *should* be. But we must remember that God was not created in our image; rather, we are created in *His* image.

You may be familiar with the Old Testament story of the Israelites making a golden calf while they impatiently waited for Moses to return from Mount Sinai. This was a god they could worship, made by their own hands and pleasing and acceptable to them. They may have found some comfort in this but it did not change who God was, or the fact that He would not compromise His holiness as they worshiped a false idol. Although we do not see many literal golden calves today, we still attempt to define what God finds acceptable based on social opinion and democracy, instead of the truth as defined in the Bible. God remains a loving God, but we cannot negotiate our way out of sin. The ordinances of His kingdom were established long before Adam and Eve and written with our best interests in mind.

Psalm 111:10 tells us, "The fear of the Lord is the beginning of wisdom," but this type of fear is not one that causes us to run from God. Rather, it embodies a holy reverence for the One who holds all things in the palm of His hand, trusting that this God who existed before the foundations of the earth will never leave or abandon us.

> He did this so that all the peoples of the earth might know that the hand of the LORD is powerful and so that you might always fear the LORD your God (Joshua 4:24).

I may have felt apprehensive about my qualifications to be in the Lord's army, but He continued to teach me that it was not about my own abilities, but my willingness to be obedient. Standing in the gateway of my greatest agony, it was *His* strength that carried me over the threshold into victory. As the leader of the armies of heaven, who sees all things and knows all things, He is my commander and I remain confident in His power and might.

> Who is this King of glory? The LORD strong and mighty, the LORD mighty in battle (Psalm 24:8).

chapter twelve

My View from the Sofa

Let the beloved of the LORD rest secure in him,
for he shields him all day long, and the one the
LORD loves rests between his shoulders.

DEUTERONOMY 33:12

Summers in Vancouver are usually lovely, one of the many reasons people refer to our province as "Beautiful British Columbia." For months we endure the cold, rainy, winter before emerging from hibernation at the first sign of spring when the crocuses show their colourful faces. Buds quickly form on the trees and within a few weeks we see leaves bursting forth. Before we know it, we are bringing our patio furniture out of storage, planting marigolds and geraniums in our flower boxes and firing up our barbeques. Vancouverites sure know how to enjoy the great outdoors! We boast that at certain times of the year we can be skiing in the morning and sailing in the beautiful bays surrounding the city in the afternoon. When sunshine finally makes an appearance, we experience an irrepressible urge to get outside and enjoy its warmth.

For me, that summer of chemo was far from fun as I spent entire days on my sofa looking out on a city that seemed to be passing me by. Initially, I experienced a honeymoon stage of not having to work everyday, but I soon felt as if I was doing jail time. I would cross out each day on my calendar, looking forward to the end of my treatment when I could get my life back in order.

As my body steadily became weaker with every round of chemo, any form of excessive noise became unbearable. At first I tried to pass the time by watching television, but even that became difficult as my eyes strained to keep up with the motion. Music seemed deafening, so I kept turning the volume down until I eventually realized that I was simply tolerating an irritation and turned it off, preferring to sit and appreciate the relief of silence. Reading became a struggle as my eyes felt as if they were being forced across each line of the page. With all my strength going into the act of reading the words, comprehension was completely compromised, so books went back up onto the shelf to collect more dust. Without the ability to sleep through the whole experience, I was completely bored and resorted to wishing my time away.

My living room is fairly small. It has one leather chair with an ottoman, a couple of side tables, and lots of books and CDs in a shelving unit with the stereo. The small gas fireplace is in the wall next to the television, and my long comfy sofa is positioned in front of a bay window, overlooking the street.

For the first ten days after every treatment I had an appointment with my sofa and the world outside my window. My activity from dawn to dusk became contemplation. I saw all sorts of cars, motorcycles, commercial vans, recreational and emergency vehicles, bicycles, pedestrians, mums with baby strollers, and kids on skateboards or rollerblades, all passing by me.

I became familiar with the deliveries for the mall across the street, garbage pickup for our block, and the Canada Post truck that passed just after eleven o'clock each morning. The progress of a building being constructed across the street also kept my attention. "My watch" was from the time of laying the foundations and pouring the cement until the delivery of windows and beginning of interior work. By watching the service vehicles that came and went, I could name off every company that had won a construction bid. Yes, the world and its citizens were carrying on all around me—they had places to go and people to meet.

My daily challenge was to make it to the bathroom without falling over. On a good day when I needed a change of scenery, I would go by way of the kitchen to get a glass of water. I developed a whole new appreciation for people with limited faculties or who were confined to wheelchairs. Only when something is taken away from us do we become aware of its value. I was humbled by the inability to do the simplest tasks. Bending down to get a new roll of toilet paper from the bathroom cupboard sacrificed precious energy, and straining to stand up again would finish me off. I began to gauge my toilet paper usage on the basis of my next expected spike in strength or scheduled visitor who could do this strenuous task for me.

Soup was one of the foods that my stomach could tolerate and was easy to prepare, so it became a staple in my diet during the first few days following chemo. This was when I reverted to survival mode, so washing dishes was never high on my list of priorities. It only became urgent when I ran out of pots and pans, although I did become very creative in how to heat a bowl of soup. To preserve my energy I would only do one thing at a time. A trip to the bathroom and then on to find my slippers would be setting the bar way too high. At least planning my day gave me something to think about.

Taking the elevator downstairs to pick up the mail was a highlight during the weekdays—an extra special treat if I opened my mailbox to find a funny get-well card waiting for me. If I was feeling adventuresome, I would make an effort to switch up my usual pyjamas, housecoat, and slippers with something a little more civilized for this big excursion. As I looked at myself in the lobby mirror, I was humbled to see a bald-headed, pale woman staring back—a woman who used to have it all together but who now struggled to get the toothpaste on the brush with some degree of accuracy.

A cycle developed following each round of chemo that generally started with two days of feeling completely drugged, when I pleadingly prayed for the room to stop moving and for strength to somehow get through the nausea. Ten days of flat-out, horizontal, down time followed as my white cell count slid off the scale along with any desire to do anything but concentrate on breathing. Then the serotonin level in my body would drop, hoisting the red warning flag that depression was about to pop out from nowhere, usually accompanied by its evil twin, loneliness.

At the end of week two I would begin an upward swing, feeling semi-normal again, just in time for the next blood test that would determine my readiness for another treatment. If my white cell count had not come back up to an acceptable range, I would have been required to take a twelve-hundred-dollar injection to speed their development. Thankfully, by the Lord's grace, that never happened.

During the many hours of contemplation and reflection, my circle of interest narrowed as my strength declined. Although I made every effort to pray for others, the Lord was literally removing my ability to do so. As I lay in a heap, completely drained, He picked me up and carried me. With my head leaning upon His chest and my arm tenderly draped over His shoulder, I felt His breath upon my face. I was not trying to set the direction or comment on the scenery; there was no discussion, just an assurance that He was taking care of me and my every need. My complete dependence upon Him literally built strength within me as my confidence was not in the ability of man, but in the power of God.

> Yours, O LORD, is the greatness and the power and the glory and the majesty and the splendor, for everything in heaven and earth is yours. Yours, O LORD, is the kingdom; you are exalted as head over all. Wealth and honor come from you; you are the ruler of all things. **In your hands are strength and power to exalt and give strength to all.** (1 Chronicles 29:11—12. Emphasis added)

In the arms of the Lord every distraction was removed. He infused truth into me as He recalled stories of great men and women of the Bible who faced huge obstacles before gaining victory.

❁ When God called Moses to lead the Israelites out of Egypt, He gave him many words of encouragement and even performed miracles for him. With every assurance from God that He would be with him, Moses' response still reflected his fears and great lack of confidence:

O Lord, please send someone else to do it (Exodus 4:13).

❁ David was anointed to be a king when he was still a young lad. His rise to the kingdom looked anything but promising as King Saul was out to take his life. While he was hiding out in caves, many lonely nights provided the substance of deep confessions from his heart. In the midst of trials and uncertainties, he still proclaimed his trust in God's mighty arm:

Some trust in chariots and some in horses, but we trust in the name of the LORD our God (Psalm 20:7).

❁ The Lord chose Joshua to succeed Moses. We read how he needed to be built up and encouraged more than once to be strong and courageous:

Have I not commanded you? Be strong and courageous. Do not be terrified; do not be discouraged, for the LORD your God will be with you wherever you go (Joshua 1:9).

❁ Esther was selected to be prepared as a queen. There is little account of her life other than one event that changed the course of history. Risking the chance of death, she courageously requested that the king reverse a decree. Her act of bravery saved an entire nation. (Book of Esther)

❁ Elijah was a great prophet of the Lord. Immediately after he had seen the awesome power of the Lord displayed on Mount Carmel, he ran away into the desert to hide because of his fears! (1 Kings 18-19)

❀ Ezekiel was sent to a people who the Lord referred to as "obstinate and stubborn," giving him advance warning of their rebellious hearts and that they would reject his message. Who would be excited over *this* commission? (Ezekiel 2)

❀ As a young boy Joseph was favoured by his father and had many dreams from the Lord. He tried to share them with his brothers, but their childhood jealousies grew into hatred towards him. This young man, whom was prophesied to rule a country, was then sold into slavery, wrongfully accused of a crime, and thrown into prison. I am sure there were many hours for reflection while he waited in his cold prison cell for his destiny to be fulfilled. Perhaps he too questioned the future that had been foretold for him. (Genesis 37–39)

Genesis 49 recounts the blessings Jacob spoke over his sons. His decree over Joseph held rich promises:

> Joseph is a fruitful vine, a fruitful vine near a spring, whose branches climb over a wall . . . His bow remained steady, his strong arms stayed limber, because of the hand of the Mighty One of Jacob, because of the Shepherd, the Rock of Israel, because of your father's God, who helps you, because of the Almighty, who blesses you with blessings of the heavens above, blessings of the deep that lies below, blessings of the breast and womb (vv.22—25).

While meditating on the richly ornamented robe that Joseph's father gave him, I likened it to the words of destiny the Lord places within us. He gives us so many rich promises that are simply beautiful, yet we are hesitant to receive them and even more challenged to hold onto them. We struggle to believe that we are worthy of such gifts. My belief is that we each have been given a cloak that has been created just for us—a heavy garment with a tapestry of our lives sewn into the background, and precious gems deepening the lustre of every gold thread, elevating its worth. The backing that supports the weight of the gems is unseen but provides strength. The fabric has been fashioned with love intertwined with hope and reinforced with courage. When I hear the voice of the Lord admonishing me to, *Awake! Clothe yourself with strength; put on your garments of splendour!* I imagine taking hold of my weighty royal cape with two hands, swinging it into the air, and allowing it to gently fall so that it rests upon my shoulders. I stand tall with confidence to face what comes my way as I have been commissioned by the King of all kings.

Through all the accounts of leaders and prophets in the Old Testament we read of their tremendous fears and lack of confidence, yet they won great victories as they trusted in the Lord. In the New Testament, Jesus and His disciples faced much opposition, yet they overcame every obstacle as they found strength in God. Courage does not mean an absence of fear but rather the determination to press on in spite of it. Acknowledging that the author of our destiny is the Lord gives us hope to believe we can and will overcome.

> For the LORD Almighty has purposed, and who can thwart him? His hand is stretched out, and who can turn it back? (Isaiah 14:27)

Nothing can thwart the plans of the Lord and He will provide for our every need!

Adding richness to my cloak is the dimension of building character through my experiences. Every challenge brings new colour and depth to the design for my life. With a desire to see cancer and its effects wiped off the face of the earth, I was reliant upon the strategies of the Lord for direction, as His is the only power great enough to annihilate it.

Since my first visit to the cancer agency I had deep aspirations to breathe life into those whose countenance reflected such sadness and grief. Unsure of how to proceed, I waited upon the Lord for wisdom. A few days before one of my regularly scheduled visits, I felt the urge to walk through the building and pray while I waited for the results of my blood test. Knowing that there is power in the prayer of agreement, I invited a friend to join me for this prayer walk.

The day before we ventured on this mission we both spent time separately in prayer, asking the Lord for strategy. We needed to be sure of the authority He was granting us to face such a large, oppressive cloud of the enemy. As we stood on the front steps of the building the next day, we were delighted to see that we had both been given the same scripture.

> Lift up your heads, O you gates; lift them up, you ancient doors, that the King of glory may come in (Psalm 24:9).

Yes, another gateway to victory!

We worked our way through every floor of the hospital, declaring the word of God and speaking hope and glory into a place that was in such desperate need of this kind of life. With our simple yet powerful prayers, we changed the atmosphere from death, to life, preparing the way for the King!

Around every corner was a confirmation of the Lord's presence. In one corridor we were greeted by a painting of an opened terrace door where beams of light filled every corner of the room. The beautiful flowers appeared to be responding to the nourishment of the sunlight, and peace was blowing through on the wings of the breeze. It seemed to embody every decree of hope that we made throughout the building.

On the face of one building we found a painting of the world, with the words, "The mystery of cancer to be revealed." No greater opportunity presented itself than this chance to pray for the mystery of God to be revealed over the nations—that His glory would cover the earth as the waters cover the sea; that individual destinies would no longer be robbed by sickness and disease but become one of promise, flowing with milk and honey and filled with hope and glory.

In the time of quietness and solitude, my view from the sofa became much more than looking out the window. My spiritual eyes and ears were opened to some of the greatest mysteries of God's kingdom, getting a glimpse of whom this Ancient of Days is, the One who rules outside of time, in a place called eternity.

chapter thirteen

An Arrow
in God's Hand

He made me into a polished arrow
and concealed me in his quiver.

ISAIAH 49:2

s my two-week cycle of sofa time would draw to a close, I became desperate to be anywhere but in my apartment. If I was having a particularly good day and was fully capable of getting dressed into something other than a track suit and slippers, I would treat myself by going out for coffee or visiting with a friend. On a couple of occasions I was even adventurous enough to tackle the big city and take in a movie. After being secluded for so long, seeing a movie was like having front row seats to a major Broadway production. My senses seemed heightened by the extended periods of silence I had endured, so the surround-sound and large screen thrilled me right down to my toes!

Hollywood has made great advances to challenge us, proving that there is always a new, creative way to express oneself or bring the pages of classic stories to life on the silver screen. I find it amazing that motion pictures with sound were only developed within the last century, and that not too long ago it was considered a major achievement to have sound synchronized with the picture! How far we have come when you consider the spectacular special effects we see in movies today.

Many years ago I volunteered to play a short role on a movie set during a tour of Universal Studios in California. I played opposite a tall, dark, and handsome man as his awestruck Lois Lane. Behind the scenes, I climbed up onto a platform and lay belly down on a support bracket that ran the length of my torso. On my left was a platform positioned a bit higher for the main man himself—Superman! Although I did not require any special wardrobe, I was happy to see that they did provide a cape for my hero. When we were in position, the crew started up the high-speed fan and simultaneously, the curtain went up. As my hair blew in the wind, Superman's cape flapped across my back, giving the appearance we were truly flying. The audience roared as the green screen behind us became a moving film showing the disappearing streets of New York as we flew higher and higher into the clouds. I could hardly contain my joy, as I was in the arms of this superhero who fights on behalf of Truth and Justice.

So much of what we experience in our lives is a mere foreshadowing of things to come—prophetic promises for those who are listening. Here I am many years later in the arms of Jesus, taking hold of the invitation to fly with Him as He establishes Truth and Justice in this world.

I have seen many icons emerge today that bear some resemblance to biblical characters or historical events. One that caught my attention was a U.S. postage stamp created a few years ago to raise funds for breast cancer research. It depicts the Greek goddess Artemis reaching back into her quiver for an arrow as she arms herself for battle. A rainbow across the sketch has been used to symbolize hope, as well as the fact that women of all colours are affected by breast cancer.

In Greece, Artemis was known as the goddess of the hunt, while the Ephesians referred to her as the goddess of fertility. She had numerous breasts (or eggs) on her chest and was notorious for great strength, earning her the label as the "defender and guardian of women in childbirth and wildlife."

The book of Acts (19:23—41) gives an account of the apostle Paul's trip to Ephesus, where he encountered great resistance from the people who stood by the goddess they worshiped.

> The city clerk quieted the crowd and said: "Men of Ephesus, doesn't all the world know that the city of Ephesus is the guardian of the temple of the great Artemis and of her image, which fell from heaven?" (v. 35).

Although the image of Artemis on the stamp is intended to empower *women* to fight for a cure, I derive comfort and confidence in knowing that *God* can do so much more than I ever could. One of the Hebrew names of God is *El Shaddai*, which means, "many-breasted one" or "all-sufficient one." One of the greatest tragedies of each generation is to omit God from the equation entirely. We are not to passively sit on the sidelines with no voice or opinion, burying our head in the sand. Rather, we are to partner with God and *His* power to find the victory.

I see my role as being honed into a very sharp, straight arrow that patiently sits in the *Lord's* quiver ready to be launched in the assault! With this thought in mind, my scroll of destiny continues to unfold before me as He teaches me what it means to be an arrow in His hand.

An arrow of precision

Over the years, numerous movies have been made about Robin Hood. What I remember most is not so much the storyline, but one exhilarating scene that was filmed from the perspective of an arrow—so exciting because it was totally unexpected. The camera was locked on a target some distance away, then *Ping!* The arrow was released and the audience was onboard for the ride. Everything other than the target was a blur as the arrow zoomed past trees on either side. The target quickly approached, growing larger and larger, and then *THOONK!* We hit the mark.

Arrows that are made of superior materials provide the greatest precision. If they are not straight, they are rendered useless. Stored in a pouch, or a quiver, on the back of a hunter, they are easily accessible to his reach. Upon spotting his prey, the skilful archer quickly plucks an arrow from his quiver and places the notch in the bowstring, slowly drawing it back as he takes aim. His eye looks down the shaft while compensating for flight distance and wind conditions. Holding his breath to steady his aim, his fingers gently release the string, launching the arrow to the desired target, confident of a direct hit. The act seems effortless and graceful as bow and arrow work in concert to hit the target.

So what does it mean for us to be an arrow in the Lord's hand? The key is to know the One who created us. He holds the blueprints.

> For you created my inmost being; you knit me together in my mother's womb. I praise you because I am fearfully and wonderfully made; your works are wonderful, I know that full well. My frame was not hidden from you when I was made in the secret place. When I was woven together in the depths of the earth, your eyes saw my unformed body. All the days ordained for me were written in your book before one of them came to be (Psalm 139:13–16).

He holds our future in the palm of His hand, and so we must listen for His still small voice and be obedient to His leading. Although we know that faith pleases the Lord, it is not the only requirement to finding Him. Most people have experienced varying degrees of hurt and rejection, so trust can be a huge hurdle. Just as in any relationship, it develops over time, so the more time we spend with the Lord in His word and in prayer, the more we get to know who He is. Understanding this God of love enhances our ability to trust all that He wants to do with us. As we begin to trust, we develop sensitive ears capable of hearing what the Spirit of the Lord is saying.

God gave me a will to forgive those I had harboured bitterness against and He healed emotions that had been shattered by disappointments. As I began to focus on Him, shackles of the past fell away and I experienced hope for the first time in years. Rainbows ushered in a new day as my face no longer stared into a dark horizon, but welcomed the light of the sun.

> Hope deferred makes the heart sick, but a longing fulfilled is a tree of life (Proverbs 13:12).

Hope is limited only by our own fears and unbelief. It is one of the great keys to life, yet we are hesitant to hope due to previous unmet expectations. Walking with the Lord is about abiding in Him or communing with Him and as we draw near, we begin to understand the mysteries of His kingdom and the path He has established for His people. As we apply all that we learn, His favour upon us is undeniable as doors seem to open with ease and all that we put our hand to prospers. A future planned by a God who loves me can be nothing short of perfect. Hope waters the dry, arid places that have previously been ravaged and written off as dead. Hope believes there will be a tomorrow. Seeds of promise begin to sprout up with a belief that abundant life is available for anyone who is thirsty—including you and I.

> For whoever finds me finds life and receives favour from the LORD (Proverbs 8:35).

The second revelation of being an arrow of God is to grasp the power of prayer. When we see the world through the eyes of the Lord, we begin to work alongside the Master. As we see a need, we draw back our bow and pray arrows of God's power and truth into the situation. We have been rooted and established in Him and walk in the authority and strength He has infused into us through His word.

> As for God, his way is perfect; the word of the LORD is flawless. He is a shield for all who take refuge in

him. For who is God besides the LORD? And who is the Rock except our God? It is God who arms me with strength and makes my way perfect. He makes my feet like the feet of a deer; he enables me to stand on the heights. He trains my hands for battle; my arms can bend a bow of bronze (2 Samuel 22:31—35).

I believe that every prayer uttered from our lips possesses the ability to change the atmosphere.

The tongue has the power of life and death, and those who love it will eat its fruit (Proverbs18:21).

If indeed we have the power of life and death in our tongue, then I venture to say that every time we open our mouth we are shooting arrows. Some may hit the mark and accomplish something wonderful. Others that hold negative words I would classify as poisonous arrows that often go about like unguided missiles doing a lot of damage before hitting their final targets. Matthew 12:36 tells us, "Men will have to give account on the day of judgment for every careless word they have spoken." I always cringe when I read this passage as many unfruitful words have passed through my lips. Often I have resolved to watch what I say, realizing the great discipline it takes to tame the tongue.

It is our choice whether we decide to speak blessings or curses, but once harmful words have been spoken, it is almost impossible to intercept and destroy them. Sometimes I have been on the receiving end of poisonous arrows, wishing the sender had fired a warning shot so I could take cover. Thankfully, we have the avenue of apology and forgiveness to heal wounds. We all know how hurtful words can be, or conversely, how a few timely words of comfort can change a person's disposition. So it makes sense that our words of prayer can also have an impact on the world around us, depending upon how each arrow is crafted.

Countless scriptures in the Bible reference prayer, but a few key passages give us the artist's rendition on how to construct arrows of precision.

> The prayer of a righteous man is powerful and effective (James 5:16).

This suggests that our spiritual posture has something to do with the effectiveness of our prayer. "Righteous" is defined as upright, moral, honest, fair, and Godly. If we possess these traits, what comes forth from our lips will reflect these qualities. If our life is steeped in immoral behaviour with little trace of Godliness, then our prayers and requests will be with selfish intentions or with judgements against those we pray for.

> When you ask, you do not receive, because you ask with wrong motives, that you may spend what you get on your pleasures. (James 4:3).

> This is the confidence we have in approaching God: that if we ask anything according to his will, he hears us (1 John 5:14).

Ah yes, there it is! We must pray in accordance with God's will—so how do we know what His will is? Jesus tells us:

> If you remain in me and my words remain in you, ask whatever you wish, and it will be given you (John 15:7).

As we continue to read His word, the Holy Spirit teaches us through revelation the many ways of God. The endless facets of His character prompt our curious nature to dig deeper for answers. Mysteries of long ago are unveiled, infusing an undeniable power called "life" and "hope" into our very DNA. Saturated with His love, our prayers begin to align with what we know of His heart. He is a

God of mercy, so our prayers naturally reflect this same sentiment as we pray for the lost. He is a God of justice, so we begin to pray for His justice to come to the poor and oppressed. He is the source of all wisdom and strength, so we petition for Godly wisdom to be bestowed upon leaders . . . and so on.

Many types of prayers exist. Some are in the form of praise and worship going heavenward; others are requests and petitions presented to the Lord on our behalf as well as others we know. Our heart gradually begins to break as the Lord's heart does for so many of His children who are in need. Other prayers sound more like war cries as we assault the powers of darkness that come against us in different arenas. There are a variety of battlefields and weapons for every type of combat. The secret is to choose the most effective weapon from your arsenal to secure the land.

Throughout the summer of my chemo treatments I attended a mentoring program that taught us how to take our prayers to a new level. We started with the ability to pray large spotlight type prayers, and then learned the fine skill of narrowing the prayer's rays to a concentrated, precise laser beam of power. On the final evening it was confirmed to me that we were indeed being prepared to be arrows in the hand of the Lord. In my state of sheer exhaustion I reached for some water and smiled as I read the brand of the bottle I had carried all season: Arrowhead™. The Lord must take great delight in watching us discover the creative ways in which He communicates with us. That evening, He confirmed to me that indeed, our prayers can make a difference.

The fourth round of chemo marked a major milestone as I had now passed the halfway point. I was promoted to a new drug called Docetaxel, which meant that I no longer needed to endure the huge vials of drugs being pushed into my veins. Even the appearance of this drug was optimistic, as it looked like a bag of water that was administered as a slow intravenous drip. Not as toxic to the veins as the previous drugs, I hoped that perhaps my body might get a break. The new drug was accompanied by a whole new set of side effects, but nothing prepared me for the onslaught of pain that worked its way through my body.

The first forty-eight hours were completely unbearable. The little unassuming clear bag of liquid had deceived me! I was unable to find a single position to sit or lay in where the pain would subside. Sleep eluded me as I attempted to escape the suffering in any way possible. Every cell in my body felt the attack of the poison, including the very centre of my soul that struggled to hold on to a will to survive. I wept with agony, unable to form the simplest of prayers. Rolling over I looked at the clock. Through my tears I could make out that it was 2:00 a.m. How many more hours of this could I endure?

"Jesus, Jesus, Jesus, Jesus . . ." Over and over I called upon the name of the One who could save me, until in a single breath I said,

"Lord, call the prayer warriors to pray for me."

I was completely spent—no strength, and very little will to live.

The next day the storm had finally passed. Although the pain had receded to a manageable level, I did not move for hours. Later that afternoon a member of my church family called to check on me and told me that a dear brother named Cyril had been awakened by the Lord at 2:00 a.m. and had prayed for me for nearly three hours. I was humbled to know that the Lord answered my prayer the moment I had asked for help and felt doubly blessed by this man's obedience to pray on my behalf.

Upon researching Docetaxel a few days later, I learned that it is made from the needles of the yew tree. The gardener for my apartment complex pointed out that these same trees line the border of our property. Interestingly, the berries from the yew tree were used in ancient times as poison in arrowheads. Merely a coincidence? Not likely. The Lord again reminded me that I would be used as an arrowhead against the enemy as I witnessed first hand the enemy's attempt to destroy me. As poison was coming against me, a fellow prayer warrior was alerted by the Lord to cover me in prayer at the very moment of this assault. His arrows reached the heavens and God in His mercy thwarted the attack.

We desperately need one another and cannot expect to survive if we go forth as lone rangers. Many times I have been awakened to pray for people, but I cannot say I persevered for three hours. I have often shot my arrow prayers and hoped for the best; not completely confident in their effectiveness and wondering if they really were making much of a difference. My new perspective has taught me to be obedient to His call and to pray with boldness and authority. I line those arrows up with thought and precision, not wanting to waste one breath, for my simple prayers may be the difference between life and death.

Many things happen in life that cannot be explained, such as why the Lord allows anyone to go through the trial of cancer. Why does He allow pain and suffering? Most of these answers will not be revealed until we reach heaven. However, we do know that the Lord promises to never leave us. As He places us in the fire, we will not be burned, but just as the dross is removed from fine metals, impurities within us will melt away. The end result does justify the means.

One thing is for certain—prayer works. If we are blessed enough to pray on behalf of another, we can move mountains. We can knock the enemy out of the garrison and take back what belongs to us.

As an arrow in the hand of the Lord, I trust completely in His strategies for this battle. I will allow Him to work out my imperfections, honing a shaft that will hold a true course when He sets me to flight. He is my superhero and with stars in my eyes I look adoringly upon the One who convinced me that this broken arrow could be repaired and was of great value.

chapter fourteen

Courage in the Valley

The eternal God is your refuge, and underneath
are the everlasting arms. He will drive out your
enemy before you, saying, "Destroy him!"
DEUTERONOMY 33:27

A s the days marched on I joyously flipped the calendar into
a new month, feeling confident that I was that much closer
to completing my "sentence." I was now familiar with the
stages of each treatment, almost able to set the clock by when the
next side affect would hit. My eyebrows, eyelashes, and hair were
completely gone. (Finally, a hairstyle that was low maintenance.)
The prescribed pills to combat pain and nausea caused my tongue
to swell until it was too big for my mouth and my teeth started
to dig into it. Sores developed in my throat and mouth, making it
impossible to eat or drink much, and any sense of taste disappeared.
Facial muscles responded with twitches, joining the involuntary
concerto being played by my finger spasms. The veins from my hands
to my elbows had been so damaged that they ached and resembled
uncooked spaghetti down the arteries of my arms. Any pressure on
my fingernail pads was painful as the nails had begun to fall off, and
every muscle and vein in my body ached, down to my toenails that

were slowly peeling away too. Going through this roller coaster of treatment once could be considered an unfortunate adventure—any more than that is almost torture.

Some of the same valleys of sadness seemed to reappear as I wished the time away. Questions, questions, and even more questions for the Lord—covering old ground of the whys and "How much longer?" Perhaps I was His impatient child who kept asking, "Are we there yet, Daddy?"

Another frustrating side effect of the drugs was an agitation that would not permit sleep. Although I was completely exhausted, my body could not settle down to find rest. I would be up at all hours of the day and night feeling like I had ingested fifteen espressos, waiting for the caffeine to wear off. Shuffling the pillows from the bedroom to the living room I would search for sermons worthy of putting me to sleep—none from my *own* pastor of course! I completed entire teaching series and moved on to books and music. Tick, tock, it was only three o'clock. In the wee hours of the morning precious sleep would finally come and my heavy eyes would find peace. However, within minutes, my sanctuary would inevitably be invaded by the loud blast of power tools from below my window.

The owner of an apartment two floors below me was completing some renovations, which included the installation of a new tile floor. He had set the power saw up on the patio, so every few moments I was assaulted by the horrific screech of the blade cutting through ceramic tile. Day after day I endured this invasive, mind-numbing noise. I began to count how many times the saw was used each hour. Calculating the number of tiles that would be required (assuming that his apartment was the same size as mine) and taking into consideration a few mistakes in cutting, I concluded that he must have tiled the walls and ceilings as well. Once the saw finally stopped, I breathed a huge sigh of relief, only to see workmen deliver the planks for trim. Admitting defeat, I mustered up enough strength to get dressed and vacate to the street below for a few hours, certain of finding a quieter venue in the bustling city than I would in my own home.

Two blocks away lay a small lake, so my mission was to summon enough energy for the round-trip journey. I took it slowly, knowing I had to preserve any speed for the two pedestrian crossings on my route. I would need to reach the curb on the opposite side of the road before the unforgiving busy traffic whizzed by me. Unwilling to waste precious strength on polite conversation or smiles at the passersby, I set my sights on a park bench and shuffled with all my might to reach it.

With only a few meters left, I lunged for the bench and collapsed in a heap on the hard seat, feeling each plank holding me up. Leaning against the rigid back, I was grateful for the armrest and glad to be in quieter surroundings. The long excursion home seemed an eternity away, giving me plenty of time to renew my energy before attempting it.

Surveying the surroundings, I spotted some Canada geese bathing in the lake. Just watching their activities exhausted me and so I lowered my head to rest. A few feet in front of me I spotted a blade of grass and fixed my gaze upon it. All I could manage in my weakened state was to watch it grow for the next thirty minutes. I reached a new low as I comprehended the full extent of my physical condition—a wet rag that had been so tightly rung out that not a drop remained, and now I was being hung out to dry.

Sometimes when the Lord does His work in us, we hardly feel his presence and experience an uncomfortable, slightly distressing, dryness. Throughout this leg of the trip I was cognizant that I needed to steer clear of negative thinking and instead, focus on the love He had for me. Some days it seemed as though the prayer was barely off my lips when it was being answered. On one occasion, my confessions of loneliness resulted in seven friends feeling the need to suddenly call or stop by in the same afternoon. Oh, the faithfulness of my Lord!

One particular day I was struggling with what to eat and did not have much on my shelves. Although I had wonderful volunteers who would willingly pick up groceries, I had no idea what I wanted or could stomach. Often, just the aroma of the wrong food could set me off. The day dragged on and still I pondered what might go down and stay down. I kept a watchful eye on the clock, hoping to catch a friend who could pop down to the store for me, until it became too late (by my self-imposed time limits) to call. It was in the middle of most people's dinner hour and I did not want to interrupt their meal just because I was not organized enough to have called earlier. At 6:30 p.m. I finally decided I would make the trip to the supermarket myself. I planned out how I could make it there, rest at the pharmacy chairs, buy some food, and return home. A quick, easy mission—no problem.

I congratulated myself on having successfully dressed in clothes that semi-matched. A bonus was to have found one of my little cancer caps that was also colour-coordinated to my outfit. There was no hair to worry about and frankly, the makeup probably would not come out of the drawer until spring.

Arriving at the store, I did not repeat a previous mistake of grabbing a carry basket that had defeated me with a few items that seemed like boulders. Instead I opted for a cart that could double as a walker in disguise. Leaning on the handle, I wheeled my way down the aisles, picking out what I needed and taking in all the sights and aromas. At this point I needed to recoup, so I worked my way over to the pharmacy department and plopped myself down in a chair to wait for a prescription that I had never ordered. After settling in I began to feel too comfortable, so decided that I should head for the checkout, preventing any possibility of falling asleep and accidentally being locked in for the night with the stock boys.

Perusing the available checkout stands, I decided upon the express checkout, hoping to be the epitome of express speed. Wasting valuable energy waiting on the person ahead of me, my impatience moved me to count the items in her basket. I needed to be assured that she had less than the allotted fifteen items, giving her the right to delay me. She passed the test and so I settled in to lean on the cart handle for the next few minutes. Her groceries slowly moved along the conveyor belt, allowing me space to unload my goodies. As I laboriously emptied my cart, one item at a time, the woman behind me suddenly caught my attention. She looked at me and with a heart of compassion said,

"I've been there."

Without hesitation, she opened her arms and asked if she could give me a hug. My tears ran down onto her shoulder as I fully embraced this act of kindness and love. For a moment it seemed like the store clerk and other customers were removed from their busyness to witness something powerful occurring. It was a lingering, genuine hug that she was fully committed to until I chose to let go.

As she proceeded to help me unpack my cart, she made light conversation and then asked if I needed a friend. I felt somewhat ashamed of myself, knowing the support network I had available, yet obviously I looked as if I was completely alone. I politely declined her kind offer to assist me with any task or to simply be someone I could call at a moment's notice.

After successfully getting myself back home, I wondered if I had once again been too stubborn (or prideful) to have accepted an offer of help. As I searched my heart, I felt the Lord simply quiet me with His love. I affectionately call that encounter "friend for a day," when the Lord provided not just an acquaintance but also a deep connectedness with a stranger, the kind that often takes a lifetime to achieve. This woman immediately reached into my heart with a sincere compassion.

The book of Hebrews tells us,

> Do not forget to entertain strangers, for by so doing some people have entertained angels without knowing it (Hebrews 13:2).

I often wonder if I should have taken her phone number.

Days like these were common. Journeying deeper into the valley of treatment, each gruelling cycle of chemo seemed to beat me down until I could no longer move. Collapsing in a heap at the end of each day with hardly the strength to speak, I was truly at the mercy of the Lord. Unable to do much in the battle, I felt that the enemy was trying to kill me; however God was simply emptying me. I did not even have the strength to argue with God or question his tactics.

After enduring the latest round of chemo that flattened me, I was unaware of all that I was suppressing until one morning I woke up feeling as if I had been punched in the mouth. To combat the pain from the drugs and their side effects, I had subconsciously begun to clench my teeth so tightly that the muscles in my jaw had completely locked up, making it nearly impossible to open my mouth—a great opportunity for me to *listen* to the Lord!

It was at this point that the Lord revealed to me that although I had been valiantly enduring my suffering, I was not *facing* it. I had felt so confident with my progress that I neglected to see that a fear of pain had crept in. The memory of that one night of excruciating pain still lingered to the point that I had become fearful of undergoing any further treatment. I only had two more rounds to go, but it seemed like far too high a mountain for me to climb.

Once again, I pondered this revelation as the Lord showed me the nature of my perseverance. Standing before me was a giant called Cancer who was too big and ugly for me to even look at. In my spirit, I had put my head down and was hoping to quickly circumvent him and the whole experience as quickly as possible. I was looking at the ground in front of me as I skirted around him, not wanting to look directly into his eyes for fear of what I might see. In a sense, I was not even fighting him as much as I was tolerating his foul smell. The Lord was directing me to *acknowledge* the presence of this giant who had my name on his lips.

Battle weary, I asked the Lord how His apostles endured the hardships that they had encountered. Paul was shipwrecked, imprisoned, beaten, stoned, and left for dead more than once. As I prayed, He took me to the book of Ezekiel and showed me numerous times when the Lord showed His mighty hand. I heard Him say, *I am Justice.* He is my advocate and fights on behalf of those who serve Him.

Just as Jesus saw what His Father did, I too, was witnessing the Lord administer His justice. As I took a stand against the principalities of darkness, the Lord's justice prevailed.

> Righteousness and justice are the foundation of your
> throne; love and faithfulness go before you (Psalm
> 89:14).

Reminding me of David's encounter with Goliath, the Lord ignited a supernatural courage within me to fully engage in this battle; to face the enemy head-on with confidence and authority. Standing to my feet, I felt the commanding presence of the Lord's power and justice behind me. My gaze gradually moved from the floor, upwards towards the eyes of the giant and I stood for a moment, acknowledging that he was after Sandra Lynn Crawford. With every ounce of strength, I proclaimed my rights as a child of God to rebuke and cast down the works of darkness. Invoking the powerful name of Jesus, I shot that devil down with the arrows of the Lord and rebuked every bit of pain that had come upon me. Finally, I cut off the head of the giant and proclaimed the victory. I did not walk around him, but ploughed over him, declaring that the enemy was now under my feet![7]

This was perhaps one of my greatest triumphs, yet it occurred in the deepest of valleys. After defeating this giant, I experienced a reality check that went beyond seeing the close proximity of the beast, to the damage he had done to which I had turned a blind eye.

> And what more shall I say? I do not have time to
> tell about Gideon, Barak, Samson, Jephthah, David,
> Samuel and the prophets, who through faith
> **conquered kingdoms, administered justice,** and
> gained what was promised; who shut the mouths of
> lions, quenched the fury of the flames, and escaped
> the edge of the sword; **whose weakness was turned
> to strength; and who became powerful in battle and
> routed foreign armies** (Hebrews 11:32–34, Emphasis
> added).

---

[7] See the Declarations of Truth in Appendix A for examples of prayers of victory.

In my weakest "blade of grass" moment, I found my strength in the Lord who continued to prove His greatness—not only showing that the battle belongs to Him and that He is victorious, but the amazing concept that He could do it through me, a simple but willing vessel.

chapter fifteen

A New Woman

Therefore we do not lose heart. Though outwardly we are wasting away, yet inwardly we are being renewed day by day. For our light and momentary troubles are achieving for us an eternal glory that far outweighs them all.
2 CORINTHIANS 4:16-17

As I travelled the road of healing, I passed road signs of encouragement and meadows of rest, full of colours of revelation that brought hope. Some stretches of road seemed to pass through the Sahara—nothing but sand as far as the eye could see. These times of loneliness and fatigue required every last drop of strength just to put one foot in front of the other and keep pressing on.

Subconsciously I had become a master of avoiding any mirrors or reflective glass, as I knew that what I would see was not pretty. One afternoon I passed too close to a mirror and was shocked and frightened to see someone peering back at me who I did not recognize. My eyes, which always seemed to exude life, appeared empty and sad, reflecting the true image of one who was completely spent with nothing left to give. As I bravely studied the image of this stranger looking back at me, I hit a new low that lurked beneath what I already thought was rock bottom.

My intent was to ignore all that was being stirred up within me, and the Lord once again prevailed as He gave me a deeper understanding of this place that teetered on the edge of the grave itself. With only one chemo treatment remaining, I was determined to close my eyes, grit my teeth and make it through—until the schedule was changed.

Since my first trip to the oncologist, I had marked all the treatment dates on my calendar, with huge stars and exclamation points on the day of my final encounter with the needle. Two days before the scheduled visit, my doctor decided to delay it for five days as I had a developed a fever. With little or no immune system, it was dangerous to proceed with another round of treatment until the fever lifted. Just when I thought that nothing more could knock me down, this unexpected punch felt like the final blow.

I had put so much hope in successfully reaching the target date that having it postponed a mere five days devastated me. Weary under the burden of disappointment, I again found myself at the foot of the cross, crying out for mercy from the Lord. My tears finally gave way to exhaustion, allowing me to grasp yet another truth of the process. I had reached a tipping point where the culmination of all my troubles, all my trials, all the pain and suffering were permitted with a divine purpose in mind. The Lord was on the verge of revealing a new woman.

> For we know that our old self was crucified with him
> so that the body of sin might be done away with, that
> we should no longer be slaves to sin (Romans 6:6).

He showed me in simple terms the process leading up to this place called the death of Sandra.

The "OLD" SANDRA was a woman of the world. Many deep changes needed to take place, as my old life had affected my character and permitted several unstable foundations within my belief system to be established. I may have repented of my sins, but the effects of them required deep, thought-provoking attention and heart-changing transformation.

Just as a spirited horse needs to be broken, I too, needed to be broken of all the selfish habits that actually worked against me. A horse must realize at some point that the trainer is on their side and can be trusted. It is the same in our walk with God. Most people would be quick in agreeing to have their selfishness removed, but they are too selfish to give it up! Instead of embracing the process, they allow bitterness and resentment to enter and begin comparing themselves to others. This can also open the door to envy and jealousy when all along, the Lord has been meticulously focussing the power of His hand upon the areas that hinder us.

During the process of stripping away, the Lord took everything out of my hands. I felt the tight rein He placed upon me, making it impossible to participate in any type of ministry that could take my focus off His work in me. He reminded me that it is His ministry, not mine. If I hoped to see any lasting reward, I must allow Him to return my work in ministry to me in *His* timing.

> Unless the LORD builds the house, its builders labour
> in vain (Psalm 127:1).

Although I welcomed the necessary work of the Holy Spirit, a part of me was crying tears of grief as I said a final farewell to Sandra. Everything of the world that I strived for and adopted as my identity was dying. This death was personal yet necessary.

Being crucified with Christ became a reality as I reflected on my experience of the past few months and the similarities to the days leading up to Jesus' death on the cross. I had been stripped naked before strangers, losing all sense of dignity; Jesus was stripped before being nailed to the cross. I suffered bodily pain far beyond anything I had ever endured before and I had been poked, prodded, and drugged. My will had been crushed and my outer appearance altered. Jesus was whipped and beaten beyond recognition. My soul was downcast with the injustice of infirmity that landed upon me; Jesus was without sin, completely innocent, yet was crucified. The difference was that Jesus died to give me life. I simply surrendered my life to Him so He could put to death those things that were not of His making.

In the empty vessel stage, I felt as if I was wandering in no man's land. The unveiling of the new woman was yet to be realized, and I was keenly aware of the Lord's sovereign protection over me as I remained positioned for an infilling of my true identity of who I am in Christ. I had often prayed "more of you Lord, and less of me," and He was taking me at my word.

I came to cherish those five days of delay as I began to see them as a turning point. Crossing over no man's land was the beginning of new life. Every cycle of treatments had been perfectly orchestrated to start another round just as I got over the previous one. However, in those five unexpected days, my body began to show signs of life again, and hope was rising within me. I treasured every extra ounce of energy and grabbed hold of the belief that I am an overcomer.

My heart began to worship the Lord with an irrepressible joy that was stirring within. All that He had revealed to me of His character was being proclaimed from my lips. This God who is gracious and compassionate towards me, who is slow to anger and who is patient and kind, showed Himself as being my teacher, my friend, my healer, a prophet who gave encouraging words, an evangelist who saved me, a shepherd who led me, and a king who reigns supreme.

The vastness of God cannot be contained, yet His mysteries can be found by those who seek Him. He is royalty revealed in majesty. He is humble yet bold as a lion, meek, gentle, and considerate. He is holy and righteous. He is justice, and vengeance belongs to Him alone. He is truth and holds the key of life. He is the source of all wisdom. He is the One that gives me strength. He is peace. He is a warrior who commands the heavenly hosts. He never surrenders and did not give up on me. He is eternal. He is confident and stands on His word. He never changes. He is revelation and knowledge. He is creative, displaying His works through signs, wonders, and miracles.

He is flawless and without sin. He is agape love, revealed in His perfect plan to save us from the grip of death. He is a sacrificial gift to sons and daughters who have become lovers of themselves, and still He professes His love for us. He has prepared for us a place in eternity, void of any striving, sickness, sadness, or suffering; a place of overwhelming peace that abounds with an endless love.

With hands raised high, these confessions of truth crept past my conscious mind to become the first trickle of glory into this empty vessel. Bowed before the king, I requested that He would entrust me with His heart—His heart for the nations, and His burden for the lost.

Souls lost, souls found

During these extra days before the final treatment, I was grateful to have an evening of entertainment, away from my regular horizontal position on the sofa. While watching a movie about the Coast Guard, I was moved by the many parallels of truth to my kingdom training. It was not just about the physically demanding circumstances that Coast Guard recruits must face, nor simply developing the skills that would qualify them for the job. Most importantly, they had to identify the core of what motivated them. Their work would put them in situations where they would have to risk their lives to save others with no time to think about it. They had to know in advance how much they were willing to sacrifice and develop the valuable quality of being able to remain calm in the midst of literal storms. The greatest hurdle seemed to be the first rescue, as that revealed whether or not they really had what it took—if all that they professed about their will and abilities held true.

I recalled my days in the Caribbean where I experienced many tropical storms and three major hurricanes. To see the devastation that wind and water can have in a very short period of time was startling. Until I had experienced it first hand, I had little regard for its power and not a small measure of pride and confidence in my own abilities. Man alone does not have the ability to contain a storm, so we must learn what to do in the midst of it. It reminded me again of how small I am, and how big God is.

As the credits rolled at the end of the movie, I was struck by the honest confessions of grief and sadness as the Coast Guard teams were compelled not to dwell on those who were saved, but instead, to remember the souls who were lost. We often focus on the souls who are saved, rejoicing in the few, perhaps in an attempt to comfort and encourage ourselves, when the truth is that many are slipping through our hands on a daily basis. The Lord impressed on me the reality of this tragedy, which further motivated my heart to beat for the lost.

Selah—pause for reflection

> You prepare a table before me in the presence of my enemies. You anoint my head with oil; my cup overflows (Psalm 23:5).

Entering into the last of my five days of grace, I felt as though I had feasted at a great banquet. I had joy and sorrows, surprises and breakthroughs, healing, understanding, and impartations. My heart was grateful for all that I was walking through—my cup overflowing with blessings.

"Coincidentally," we had two altar calls that Sunday at church. The first was a commitment to lay all that we had before the Lord in complete surrender (emptying ourselves), and the second followed the pastor's message on "knowing your identity in Christ."

> But you are a chosen people, a royal priesthood, a holy nation, a people belonging to God, that you may declare the praises of him who called you out of darkness into his wonderful light (1 Peter 2:9).

I gratefully accepted the truth that I am the Lord's beloved daughter, whom He has chosen for His kingdom.

The Lord in His great faithfulness provided a tangible confirmation of this great banquet as I visited a woman I had met at the cancer agency. Her family observed a different faith, but we found common ground in our battle against cancer. They graciously received me into their home and proceeded to bring out all kinds of food and drink during our brief time together. Making my way home, I pondered the miracles of the past few days. Already I sensed the infilling of His glory and felt honoured to be chosen as one of His precious saints. In the heat of that summer day, He once again revived the hope of my future. I was called with a purpose, prepared by the King, for the King—a woman of royal destiny.

chapter sixteen

Navigating the Minefield

Whether you turn to the right or to the left,
your ears will hear a voice behind you, saying,
"This is the way; walk in it."

ISAIAH 30:21

Throughout the journey up into the mountains and down into the shadowed valleys, I was continually reminded of the redemptive qualities of the cross. If I was not directly battling a giant, I could sense its closeness and was grateful to have God on my side. On ordinary days of simple survival, I successfully remained hidden from the enemy and was pleased to be placing my head on my pillow late in the evening with one more day behind me. In the flurry of chaos, a quiet day was often a welcome relief and a new opportunity for the Lord to present me with a deeper revelation of who He is in the midst of it all.

With only one chemo session remaining, I was beginning to feel like a seasoned veteran, confident in knowing the battleground and seemingly assured of a victory. Summer had ended and Canadian Thanksgiving was just around the corner. I was blessed to be invited to a research company's focus group for women who had battled breast cancer and considered it a great opportunity to give back to the community through my candid confessions. The intention of the group was to obtain first-hand information from those who had gone through chemotherapy, gathering relevant feedback on a proposed alternate treatment. Although I was lying low, I was curious and feeling somewhat adventuresome, so decided to make the effort to get myself into town that evening.

As we gathered in the boardroom, we engaged in light conversation, getting acquainted until a company representative sat down and outlined the meeting directives. Four participants were present, all of whom at one time or another had been treated for breast cancer. Two of us were still undergoing chemo. As the evening unfolded, the Lord revealed the depth of His grace that I had been walking in. I was truly humbled to realize how I had taken it for granted.

So much within my heart was stirring as each woman confessed the trials they had endured throughout their treatments. I began to see that every level of pain I had endured since the outset had prevented me from recognizing the unparalleled extent of His protection, provision, favour, and grace towards me.

One woman described the abandonment and inconsistency she experienced when she was shuffled from one oncologist to the next due to unusual circumstances. She recounted how the initial regime of drugs did not work, so they had to start again. More than once she was faced with spending twelve hundred dollars for a supplementary injection when her blood count did not return to the required level before proceeding to the next round of chemo. I listened to stories of husbands who did not help out and children who needed to be cared for, not understanding why mommy was sick. Some described chemo treatments that were so gruelling that their teeth fell out. One woman had not been given any assurance that the cancer had not spread, as no additional tests had been ordered. Another woman required a drug that was not yet covered by the provincial medical plan and so had to lobby the government to get the drug before she could proceed. As one hour rolled into the next, I sank further into my chair, speechless as I listened to these horrible experiences.

With every confession of their pains and trials, the grace of God became increasingly magnified within my heart. I could not wait to utter words of apology to the Lord for so willingly receiving from His hand while neglecting to be grateful for His extraordinary care. As I drove home in quiet contemplation, He reminded me of the details He had attended to on my behalf. With every powerful prayer I had uttered, each swing of my sword to combat the enemy, the Lord had dispatched a thousand angels to wage war in the unseen battle.

He had assigned me to one of the best surgeons in the world and to an oncologist who was personally involved in my treatment. In what I now see as an unusual gesture, my oncologist had not hesitated to give me her home phone number should I have needed to contact her. As the women recounted how pleased they were to have had a doctor spend half an hour with them, I recalled the four-hour visit with mine. I remembered all the additional x-rays and scans that were ordered to eliminate any question of the state of my bones and core organs. I had seen it as an inconvenience, but God had ordered it to silence the voice of the tormentors.

My initial regime of eight treatments of chemo had been changed to a hotter mix that reduced the number of sessions to six. I had been so afraid of the higher dosage that I did not give much attention to the sovereign work of the Lord's hand to have knocked two months off my treatment time. Not once did I have to pay for extra prescriptions, nor did I have any financial worries for an entire year. I continually witnessed the miracle of my blood count going well above the required minimum levels, which prevented me from any delays.

I recalled the supernatural favour I received when on one occasion I ended up in the emergency room with a high fever. Since my body did not have the resistance to fight any kind of infection, I had been warned to go to the hospital should this occur. When checking in, the nurses immediately attended to me, setting me up in a private room where they ran every possible test to determine the source of the infection.

I was never short of volunteers to take me to appointments, or friends to lift me up through cards, gifts, and heartfelt prayers. I had the best of care and knew I was never alone or abandoned. Although my pain had been challenging, it could have been so much worse if I had not been walking with God.

As I meditated on my many blessings, He reminded me of my willingness to serve Him when I had said, "Here I am Lord, use me." He showed me a picture of a minefield and revealed that the road of redemption for this particular burden had been harder than others. In order to claim the total redemption for breast cancer, it required a dangerous walk through a minefield on the way to the cross. He allowed the journey of redemption to be in my generation, and upon me.

I grappled to understand this rockier road of redemption, wondering why it was even necessary. Why did all this have to occur? Could I not have just offered a heartfelt prayer of repentance and been done with it? In response to all my questions, He showed me another picture and likened the cancer to a dandelion. Being a gardener I was very familiar with this stubborn weed that is difficult to eradicate from any garden. If any part of the root is not removed, each broken piece springs up into a new weed. He showed me that in order to conquer every last bitter root of cancer, I needed to walk through this field with a repentant heart postured towards Him to seek and destroy every part of the root.

> His [Jesus] sheep follow him because they know his voice. But they will never follow a stranger; in fact, they will run away from him because they do not recognize a stranger's voice (John 10:4-5).

He has trained me to be obedient to His voice, which inevitably led to a path of safety past hidden traps and snares of the enemy. Under his guidance I had located every last tentacle of cancer in me and nailed it to the cross—the source of all redemption and healing. He had prepared me for this mission as a U.S. Navy SEAL, the special operation commandos who live by the conviction that "failure is not an option." Their rigorous training, which often lasts for years, could be for one life-changing, nation-saving assignment. Reflecting upon all the deep work that the Lord had done within me, I came to appreciate the SEALS belief that "the more you sweat in peacetime, the less you bleed in war."

As my mind wandered back to the boardroom, my heart was moved by the sorrow the Lord must have felt as we heard the confessions of the only Jewish woman amongst us. She proudly recounted how she had invited three high-ranking religious representatives of three different faiths to come into the operating room with her to pray over the proceedings. Sadly, she had not chosen someone who represented the one God who had the power to make a difference—her Messiah, the Holy One of Israel who calls her the apple of His eye, Yeshua, Jesus; her Abba, the Father who longs to have her enter into the unfailing love that awaits her.

Shelter in the wilderness

> Open for me the gates of righteousness; I will enter
> and give thanks to the LORD (Psalm 118:19).

The Lord's timing is always perfect. Thanksgiving weekend came two days after the focus group, in which He caused me to *see* His goodness, blessings, and grace. Coincidentally, the Jewish Feast of Tabernacles[8] fell on the same weekend, giving me a double portion opportunity for giving thanks.

I was so filled with gratitude for all that the Lord had done for me and all that was yet to be fulfilled. As Thanksgiving is a time to celebrate the harvest, I rejoiced in the harvest He had measured out for me. I rejoiced in the seed He continually placed in my hands and the Godly wisdom and strategies He had imparted. My season of preparation had not yet been complete, but the boundary markers had been established for an appointed time. I celebrated my freedom from captivity and the provision the Lord made for me while I was

---

[8]   A Jewish festival that commemorates the shelter of the Israelites during their forty years in the wilderness.

in the wilderness. Again, songs of joy came forth from these lips as I worshiped the one true God of the universe, maker of the heavens and the earth—my kinsman redeemer, Jesus, who bought me with a price. Only by what was accomplished on a cross two thousand years ago did I qualify to draw near to God, who is an all-consuming fire. He is Holy and I am blessed and honoured to be called one of His children.

I will proclaim His goodness to the nations; I will tell of His exploits. I will say He is mine and I am His and His love endures forever. The overflowing goodness from heaven will be deposited wherever my feet tread. My hands will bless those who are hungry to know this unfailing love. I cannot out give Him and I cannot outrun Him. Even when I am sleeping, He is working on my behalf, this God who never slumbers. I am blessed and highly favoured under the gentle care of this Good Shepherd. I cannot escape the irrepressible, undeniable love and blessing and favour of this wonderfully magnificent, all-encompassing God: Jehovah Jireh, my provider; Jehovah Rapha, my healer; Jehovah Nissi, my banner; Jehovah Tsid-Kenu, my righteousness; Jehovah Shalom, my perfect peace; Jehovah Shammah, the One who is everywhere, in all things. This is my great King of glory, the Lord of all the heavenly hosts who is strong and mighty in battle.

Just as Israel pauses to celebrate the provision of their God during their forty years in the wilderness, I too, took time to celebrate the faithfulness of the Lord in the land of the living. Guided by His loving hand, I successfully navigated through a minefield of hazards, to the place of victory, life and joy.

> Do not grieve, for the joy of the LORD is your strength (Nehemiah 8:10).

chapter seventeen

Restoring the Vision

Where there is no vision, the people perish.
PROVERBS 29:18 KJV

I have always admired those who take an idea or concept and make it a reality. The advancement of technology is proof of these great pioneers who have fostered a vision by taking great leaps of faith in bringing it to life.

We often hear the stories that describe Abraham as a great man of faith, but we hear little about his wife Sarah, other than the fact that she laughed at God when she heard Him say that she would give birth to a son in her old age. I confess I am a lot more like Sarah, as I often struggle to embrace and believe all of God's great plans for my life. Instead of answering with a resounding, "Yes, God!" my questioning heart responds with comments that undoubtedly begin with "Me? Seriously?" My mind becomes the first stumbling block to embracing the dreams.

Just before my final chemo, I experienced a crisis of faith as I began to wonder what was next. What was I going to do with the rest of my life? With great anticipation I was standing on the threshold of my destiny, yet I was still surrounded by fatigue on every side that would delay my advancement. What had the Lord prepared for me and what had He prepared me *for?*

A very timely birthday gift came my way that began to dispel the mountain of fears and anxieties—a beautiful plaque that carried an assuring promise:

> I will instruct you and teach you in the way you should go; I will counsel you and watch over you (Psalm 32:8).

The Lord in His faithfulness knew the weight of this burden to know more, so continued to give me this verse from different sources for an entire week. "Coincidentally," a good friend called to discuss plans for his company, plans that included me as part of his team. Although I was running ahead of the Lord, He still delighted in answering my questions, reminding me that He had never left His post—He had everything under control.

As the next chapters of my life began to unfold, I realized how ignorant I had been when I first volunteered for God's army. After the honeymoon stage of our relationship, I endeavoured to live in the supernatural, and then was struck square in the face with a dose of reality. I had been wooed by God's love and received so many wonderful words and promises about my future that I ventured to put them into practice the next day—book me on the next flight to China! When I decided I wanted to save the world, I had no concept of the deep level of preparation that was so necessary before stepping out the front door. Over time, my hopes and dreams steadily faded into obscurity.

This season in the refiner's fire was unlike any other I had experienced. Unable to see the big picture, my only hope had been to put my complete trust in the Lord. It is said that in the process of refining silver, timing is crucial to achieve success. The silversmith is so skilled in his craft that he knows precisely when the process is complete. When he can see his reflection in the dross-free shine of the precious piece of silver, then he pulls the burning metal out of the flames. My prayer is that I will continue to grow in the likeness

of Jesus with every trial I endure so my countenance will reflect who
He is.

> Unless a kernel of wheat falls to the ground and dies,
> it remains only a single seed. But if it dies, it produces
> many seeds (John 12:24).

Many times the Lord has highlighted this verse to me as He helped me
understand the reason for my struggles. Often, I was quick to blame
every bad day on assaults from the enemy, when in fact the Lord was
accomplishing some of His greatest work in me, by *allowing* the enemy
to agitate me. He was showing me how important it was for the master
gardener to prune me, removing my selfish ways and making me more
fruitful. I began to witness the transformation in my character as the
Lord gently stripped away the "old" Sandra. Just when I thought He
was ready to put down the pruning shears, He nudged me to perform
one last act of surrender. My visions for the future had to be laid down;
they too, had to die so they could be resurrected with truth.

The Lord reminded me that we can often become so focused
on *our* idea of how to accomplish God's work that it consumes us
and becomes an idol of sorts. Often, the more we strive to build a
ministry, the less likely we are to remember that it is His plan and
that He runs the show. I am sure that God *appreciates* our eagerness
to help Him out and *enjoys* hearing all our ideas on how He should do
things, but the truth is He does not *need* any advice from us! I often
envision Him patting me on the head saying, *You just keep telling me
what your plans are and we'll see how far you get with that. We'll talk
again later when you run out of steam, little one.*

On the morning of my final chemo, I again met with the Lord at
the communion table and awaited His fresh word for the day:

> He makes his angels winds, his servants flames of fire
> (Hebrews 1:7).

I thought back to my trip to Wales during the one-hundredth

anniversary of the Welsh Revival. My spirit had been stirred when I visited the places where the great revivalist Evan Roberts had preached. Standing on the soil where they once had experienced a great outpouring of the Holy Spirit, I was moved to make declarations that the Lord's truth and mercy would again be poured out upon His people. Having read the account of how the revival died, I prayed in repentance for those the enemy had used to shut Evan down and asked the Lord to redeem all the seeds that He had sown long ago. In that moment I felt a torch was being placed in my hand to carry this same message of God's love—to be a flame of fire igniting the hearts of His people. Although I surrendered this vision with all the rest, the Lord was giving it back to me as a gift, a hope on this final day of treatment.

As I entered the hospital for one last dose, the fog was beginning to lift and I was once again finding my purpose. Claiming my seat by the window, I settled into the familiar chair and braced myself for a last shot of poison. After the first thirty minutes, a woman entered the room with some trepidation. Following close behind was a companion who fit the profile of the patient's driver—someone who carried all the coats and bags, was not sure of the routine, and deferred to the needs of the patient. The nurse began to go over the procedure with her and I correctly discerned it was her first treatment. Thinking back to my first experience in the chair, I remembered my fears and the unsettling affirmation from another patient who described the first time as the worst.

So many months before I had been paralysed in the surgeon's office, knowing I could not instill hope in another patient as I had hardly begun my own journey. Now, I was a voice of experience that had something constructive to say—tangible promises of a life that would be transformed within a few short months.

For the rest of my session I prayed silently, asking the Holy Spirit for wisdom on how to approach this woman. She was fragile, and I did not want to hurt or offend her at such a vulnerable time. When I was finally free of the needles and tubes, I mustered enough strength to push myself up onto my feet, then slowly approached her. By now she was surrounded by her driver, the nurse, and a friend who had stopped by.

Introducing myself, I asked if I could speak to her for a moment. With no extra chairs available, I knelt down and took her free hand in mine. She looked right into my eyes as I began to impart hope and encouragement for her journey. The Holy Spirit filled my mouth with the appropriate words to tell her of my own experience. I painted the picture of courage, strength, and hope that she would have the opportunity to discover along the way and assured her that she could overcome fears as she faced every giant that comes against her. I recounted the story of Moses, when the Lord placed him on a hilltop as the armies fought below. As long as his arms were raised, they would conquer the enemy. When he grew tired, he was unable to hold his arms up for the duration of the battle and so his two companions helped him. I reminded her that there were many who loved her and wanted to be of assistance, and that it was okay to invite them in as allies.

Treading carefully, I continued to speak directly to her heart. I asked if she was familiar with the *Footprints* poem and she nodded, "Yes." From my back pocket I pulled out a small card with a portion of the poem printed on it.

"I have had this on my dining room table for the past six months," I said. "Today I felt the Lord nudging me to put it in my purse, as there was someone He had in mind who needed to hear this promise today."

As the nurse got up and walked towards her station, I hesitated, thinking I may have offended her. However, she quickly returned with a box of tissues as the three of them were welling up with tears. Before placing the card in the woman's hand, I gently reminded her that Jesus knows what it is to suffer and knew the intimate details of all that she was enduring. He would never leave her and would carry her when she was unable to stand. Through all her tangled hoses, she reached down to embrace me as a natural response to the love of Jesus—the One who would carry her through.

Making my way to the elevator, I felt honoured to have had the opportunity to speak into her life, to be chosen as the messenger to deliver a life preserver of hope.

The road ahead of me was suddenly becoming brighter as I witnessed the handiwork of God. Many times I would sing songs of praise and worship to Him, confessing my willingness to walk in His ways on the path He had laid out for me. From the sanctuary I would sing, "I surrender all," and then gingerly return to the deeply entrenched habits of "leaning on my own understanding." As He watched me master the technique of peeling my clenched fingers off my selfish desires, I experienced extraordinary grace and the unquenchable fire of His love. After laying everything before Him, my aspirations remained dormant for a period of time until finally, new life began to spring up. Some of my lost dreams were being returned and the flame of hope for old promises rekindled. I had made it through the fire and what remained were the gifts and callings that were of His making, not mine.

It was November and our church was hosting a women's conference. The theme was Isaiah 54.

> "Sing, O barren woman, you who never bore a child; burst into song, shout for joy, you who were never in labour; because more are the children of the desolate woman than of her who has a husband," says the LORD (v.1).

This scripture had become very dear to me as a promise for something more than just dry and barren land; something more for a woman who never bore a child. One evening when we were praying about the meetings, the Lord said that I was a Sarah of this generation. I had laughed at God when He said He could bring something forth through this vessel. I began to weep as He laid upon my heart the disappointments of so many women who were stuck in the desert, unable to believe that they could be used for great exploits. As I asked the Lord's forgiveness for our unbelief, a desperate cry reached heaven with tears of grief for all that the enemy had robbed from us. As I lay prostrate before the Lord, He responded with songs of joy bursting forth from my belly and I was finally free of the snare I had been entangled in for years. He revealed the hope of my calling and unveiled a vision that I could finally believe.

chapter eighteen

Blueprints for Victory

The weapons we fight with are not the weapons of the world. On the contrary, they have divine power to demolish strongholds.
2 CORINTHIANS 10:4

The next step towards recovery was a few weeks of radiation. This is where high doses of concentrated energy beams are pointed directly to the area where the cancer had initially been discovered. If any trace of cancer remained after the chemo, the radiation would completely destroy it. I was not familiar with the procedure but felt confident that it would be much easier than chemotherapy.

Accuracy is vital, so little black or blue dots are tattooed onto the skin, pinpointing the boundary markers for radiation. This simplifies the technician's task of lining the machine up on every visit. The tattoos did not worry me. I had just been poisoned for four months, so what was the big deal with a couple of little dots?

At the preliminary session, the nurse began by warning me of all the possible side effects of radiation. *Here we go,* I thought, *I can expect those fiery arrows to come out of her quiver anytime now.* Sure enough, I heard about everything from irritated skin to severe burns and blisters, delivered with a distinct machine-gun approach—"rattatatta-tatta-tat!" with no seeming consideration for the patient. We then watched a short video presentation explaining the entire procedure, which was quite helpful and less intrusive, but nevertheless, left me emotionally drained.

From there we moved into the "tattoo parlour." I had this image of a rather large tough guy wearing a t-shirt three sizes too small for him, sitting upon a stool that only supported one cheek. He would adjust the magnifying glass and spot lamp, preparing to create a work of art. Leaning in, he would draw a beautiful, awe-inspiring dot with the very delicate artist's-type needle in his hand. Everyone in the room probably heard the little dream cloud above my head pop as I walked into the drawing room.

Two nurses dressed in white lab coats brought in a well-used plastic tool box that resembled something I had seen in a preschool to organize paints and brushes, complete with permanent spillage marks all over the sides. They each matter-of-factly donned a pair of plastic gloves and grabbed a huge pin to make their mark.

After being unsuccessful with the first jab on my chest, they gave it another couple of goes until they were satisfied. The process was repeated with a jab on my back. Then they slathered a generous amount of ink over the holes and with a large messy rag, wiped up the excess, leaving me to clean up the remaining stains at home. The trauma I suffered from this insignificant visit, surprised me. I sensed that I had been marked by the enemy and was bleeding black and blue ink to confirm the hit.

Arriving home I again found myself at the feet of Jesus, asking him to lift the residue of this traumatic event from me. As I sat before Him in silence, He seemed to be preparing me for what was to come. There was a kindness to the conviction of having terribly abused my skin in the past. As a young girl I had always coveted a deep tan in order to look more attractive and more times than I can remember, I unintentionally burned my skin to the point of blisters. I would often go to tanning salons to get a base before heading to warm destinations, where I again subjected my skin to the harmful rays of the sun with little or no lotion. Here I was asking for help through this next leg of the journey when I would be subjected to high doses of radiation, yet was guilty of having voluntarily done this most of my life. Now *having* to do it put a different perspective on its ability for destruction. My friend Jesus again picked me up and cleansed me as I came before Him in prayer, thankful for the awesome privilege to call upon Him day or night.

On the heels of believing I was on my way back up the mountain, here I was again, flat out before Him in tears, learning yet another lesson. In typical fashion, the Lord encouraged me as He began to show me what He had placed in my hands—the arsenal of weapons I was to use against the enemy, and the Lord's strategies for engagement. Although I often felt weak with all my tears, He reminded me that He can use a broken spirit and a contrite heart (Psalm 51:17), and that in my weakened state, He is strong. He revealed that two of the most powerful weapons we can use to attain victory is the word of God and prayer. I have always been a firm believer in the power of prayer, but did not always understand or appreciate the different levels of effectiveness we can achieve.

I began with a simple understanding that prayers are a conversation with God. They do not have to be fancy, but our sincerity does invite more response from Him than hollow words. Many people lay their requests before God but go no further in their relationship with Him, perhaps due to a lack of understanding, or just a contentment to stay where they are. Nothing is *wrong* with this approach, but so much more awaits those who are hungry.

As my relationship with God developed, I began to see that I responded differently to each part of the Trinity. I now see the heavenly Father as the perfect Dad who loves me even when I mess up—the kind of Father who welcomes me upon His knee no matter how old I am. Jesus, the Son, is whom I run to first when I need a friend. I relate to Him easier because He came in human form and looks just like us—or do we look like Him? And finally, the Holy Spirit is one I often take for granted because I find it difficult to form an image of how a Spirit should look. I am constantly reminded that the Holy Spirit is my counsellor and guide. This is how the power of God lives and moves and breathes.

Shifting from conversational prayers towards arrow prayers was a gradual progression that developed from sheer practice and a willingness to learn. Mentors were so valuable (and so necessary) when I was exercising my spiritual wings. I would watch and learn from those who had gone before me and who walked in great authority over the powers of darkness. The Lord had trained their hands for war and they had earned each promotion.

There is order and structure in His kingdom for our protection. If the Lord entrusted me with a level of authority and power beyond my understanding, the enemy would snatch it right out from under my nose due to my lack of experience. Have you ever wondered why some people seem to get their prayers answered and others do not? It has nothing to do with favouritism, but everything to do with the authority they have been given by the Lord. The anointing of God comes with a price, which inevitably includes personal sacrifice. There are many generals of prayer that I have come to respect, knowing that their armour must have nicks and dents that could tell some stories.

One of those generals is Dutch Sheets, a respected teacher who has written some valuable books on prayer. During my divinely appointed sofa time, the Lord revealed a new strategy to me for spiritual battles as I listened to Dutch Sheets on *It's a New Day*, a popular Christian TV talk show in Canada. He was discussing the power of our words and the ability to change the atmosphere around us.

> For the word of God is living and active. Sharper than any double-edged sword (Hebrews 4:12).

He explained the simple truth that as we establish the Lord in areas of influence in our lives, His government and authority will reside there. We need to be listening to the Holy Spirit and paying attention so we can exercise and proclaim the truths of His word to make a difference.

By tolerating delays and stumbling blocks, we fall into the trap of underestimating the enemy's assignments against us. When we assume that these blockades are just part of life, we have devalued the position the Lord has given us. If your assignment is to fly across the nation to pray for a dying friend in a hospital bed, do not be surprised if the enemy delays the plane just to keep you away from saving one more soul. We have been tolerating the enemy long enough!

As I continued to take in this fresh perspective on my authority, I heard the whisper of the Lord say *Dutch Blitz*. I did not think much of it until the next day, when I was browsing the sale table at my favourite bookstore. Right before my eyes was a card game called "Dutch Blitz." Now the Lord had my attention.

> The dictionary defines "blitz" as:
> intensive attack; damage; destroy; violent campaign intended to bring about swift victory.

A blitz is a military tactic based on speed, surprise, and co-ordination. Troops do not stop to celebrate a victory, but carry on with the next assault.

I continued to get confirmations of this new strategy for me as I watched our B.C. Lions professional football team desecrate their opponents to win the championship Grey Cup that year. (I confess I only become a fan during the playoffs, so it takes a few plays before I really understand what is going on.) Imagine my surprise when the announcer described the tackle as a blitz!

So often I would allow the enemy to push me back, knock me down, and put me in a corner, but no more! A shift took place as I grasped the truth of the authority that I had been given to tear down the strongholds of the enemy. I could change the atmosphere to usher in God's presence, no longer being pushed back but moving from a position of defence into one of *offence*.

> Praise be to the LORD my Rock, who trains my hands
> for war, my fingers for battle (Psalm 144:1).

After safely storing this strategy in my kit bag, the Lord then situated me in a posture of "standing".

Therefore put on the full armour of God, so that when the day of evil comes, you may be able to stand your ground, and **after you have done everything, to stand** (Ephesians 6:13. Emphasis added).

Everywhere I turned, the word STAND was staring right back at me. There comes a time when we have fought the enemy, proclaimed the truth, and yet he persistently tries to beat us down.

Submit yourselves, then, to God. Resist the devil, and he will flee from you (James 4:7)

In this final posture of standing, the enemy will inevitably try to steal the strength that is keeping you upright—your faith. Faith in the promises, faith in the Lord's plan, faith in knowing you have not been abandoned, and faith to believe you have won the victory.

The very fact that the Lord directed us to put on armour assures us that we will be involved in battles that are not at a distance, but up close and personal. As I pondered this act of standing, the Lord gave me a vision of the ceremonial guards outside Buckingham Palace in London, who stand perfectly still and are not permitted to move or be affected by the tourists around them. I have often wondered how they are able to endure the annoyance of people who make it their personal mission to distract them—jumping up and down and trying to stare them down. I marvel at their ability to stay calm and remain completely unmoved by the activity around them.

The Lord taught me that it can feel just that annoying when the enemy gets in our face with his mocking words and accusations, intending to be irritating with every move he makes.

Let us be self-controlled, putting on faith and love as a breastplate, and the hope of salvation as a helmet (1 Thessalonians 5:8).

Withstanding this test of faith in the face of the enemy's assaults positions us to be overcomers.

> For everyone born of God overcomes the world. This
> is the victory that has overcome the world, even our
> faith (1 John 5:4).

Even though my body was in a weakened state, I fixed my eyes upon the Lord and believed in the miracle of this transformation that was taking place on the battlefield.

Remembrance Day (November 11) was just around the corner, a day dedicated to the memory of all those who fought in wars for the pursuit and defence of liberty. Each year veterans proudly display their medals, many having endured deplorable conditions in far away lands and making sacrifices that the rest of us cannot even imagine. As one soldier amongst vast armies of troops, it must have been challenging to keep fighting when the overall picture was only known by the commanders.

In this battle against breast cancer I had not earned any medals, but I did hold an arsenal of weapons I was prepared to use against my adversary the next time he got in my face. I did not see the big picture, but knew and trusted the One who does.

As the Lord rolls out the blueprints for battle, the banner of victory flies over each one He calls His own. We too are soldiers who fight for liberty and freedom, establishing the kingdom of heaven, carrying the baton that the generations before us also carried, freeing prisoners from the captivity of darkness, and giving life to those who are dying.

> With God we will gain the victory, and he will trample
> down our enemies (Psalm 108:13).

chapter nineteen

Shell-Shocked

A thousand may fall at your side, ten
thousand at your right hand.

PSALM 91:7

For months I had been anticipating this day, my final radiation treatment that marked the end of the massive battle against breast cancer in my body. Chemo was over and now the long-awaited last radiation hurdle was behind me as I crossed the dreadful day off the calendar. After nine long months I had lined up celebratory meals with friends, but sadly nothing within me wanted to celebrate. If anything, I just experienced a satisfying sense of relief as I quietly crossed the finished line. No waving of large banners or dancing—simply a sigh and acknowledgement of a time to recoup. After months of holding my breath, not knowing what was around the next corner, I could gratefully exhale and assess the damage that resulted from this war.

It was only a week before Christmas, so I busied myself with the season's preparations. I was aware of a cloud that was over me—a dullness that I simply explained away as being too much to do before Christmas with little or no energy. Still, I could not escape the disturbing conflict I sensed in wanting to celebrate this magnificent milestone, yet possessing no spark or desire to jump for joy. I likened it to the shell-shocked soldiers that return from the battlefront. They cannot wait to get home but when they arrive, the shock of what they have been through finally hits them. The world around them has not changed, but they have. There is also a sense of gratefulness of being one who survived.

I felt lonely in this state of mind as nobody, including me, really understood what I was going through. Encouraging words from those around me seemed shallow, as something within the darkest recesses of my soul was blocking the joy of victory—we were not done yet. The doctors told me that my reaction was normal, something that every cancer patient experiences and that I would eventually get over it. They referred to it as being in limbo—that "in between" stage that leaves you trying to pick up the pieces of what is left of your life. I was learning that the transition between war and peace is a journey in itself.

I had completed my scheduled assignments; every doctor's appointment, scan, blood test, x-ray, and treatment. It was an underwhelming finish to all that I had been directed to endure . . . And now what?

When can I go back to work?

What kind of job will I look for?

I am really tired, so how am I going to be able to keep up?

I cannot walk up a flight of stairs without needing a nap. How long is it going to take to get over this?

Who's going to hire a tired cancer patient?

When will my hair grow back so I do not have to wear hats all the time?

The questions were unending, making me weary just *thinking* about tackling my future.

Although this stage was considered normal, I wrestled with the Lord over it. I read a couple of books that confirmed my sense of being a bit lost, but they did not really help. I met with one of our prayer team members and as we prayed through it, the Holy Spirit whispered the word, *trauma.*

Trauma carries many emotions with it including grief, fear, weariness, and condemnation. There was such a confirmation within my soul when we stumbled upon the solution. In my mind, I had great guilt over feeling that I should be getting back to work right away because the treatments were finished. Sadly, many who had not walked this road seemed to agree, subtly inquiring why I was not doing more. They pressed me to answer questions about my immediate future while I was just beginning to believe that I *had* a future. The enemy had made a direct hit at my weakness of "needing" to work, thereby bringing me under great condemnation to get back behind the desk just days after the final radiation beam had been administered. My mind and will were expecting so much more from this tired body that had just escaped death.

I took stock of how my body had fared these past nine months and realized that quite a few wounds still needed time to heal. My hair was nothing more than some peach fuzz beginning to poke through. It seemed to be predominantly grey with a bit of black—quite different from my usual brunette. My eyebrows and eye lashes were starting to grow back in a wild, haphazard way, needing a gentle reminder of where they should sit. A couple of veins in my left arm had not recovered from the toxicity of the chemo and remained sensitive and painful to touch. I was reminded of their lack of elasticity every time my arm moved. My right arm was recovering well but was still numb around the area where the incision had been made to remove the lymph nodes. My fingernails and toenails had completely fallen off, leaving my fingers tender and susceptible to cuts.

Perhaps the greatest surprise for me was how long it took me to recover and get back in shape. I had unrealistically expected to get right back in the saddle of my life—a common assumption for cancer survivors. Never one to admit I could not do something, it was humbling to start rehabilitating my body from the beginning. Standing for any length of time was taxing, as was the simple action of getting up from a squat or sitting position. It was not until I received some simple, honest counsel from a friend that I understood I felt defeat and shame about the shape of my body once again. She simply said, "Keep at it and the body will respond." Her encouraging words of truth dispelled every bit of discouragement I was experiencing due to my failure to reach the high bar I had set for myself. I reset workout goals that were attainable and no longer felt ashamed about choosing the three-pound weights instead of the huge ten- and twenty-pound dumbbells.

Free of self-imposed judgments, my first goal was to sign up for a fitness program. I joined a gentle swim class for those with limited mobility—another blow to my pride as I was forced to admit my "disability." Donning a swim suit when I was completely out of shape and still nearly bald was the last thing I wanted to do, but at this point I had little or no dignity left. At least I did not have to strip down to the waist and put on a hospital robe! It was wonderful to be in the water again and the exercises proved to be the perfect solution to gently wake my muscles up. I progressed to doing more cardio and strength training in a gym, isolating the different muscle groups in an effort to bring them back to life.

For weeks after my final session, my body reflected the effects of the poison. I was surprised that my legs experienced the greatest long-term side effects from the chemo. The last drug administered to me targeted the bone marrow, rapidly depleting the calcium, which explained all the aches and pains that followed. All strength was robbed from the muscles in my legs, causing them to feel like gelatin when doing the simplest activity. Climbing up and down stairs and getting up off chairs was particularly difficult. The challenge was to know my limit, which I usually identified long after I had passed it.

Often I went for short walks and found myself completely fatigued after two or three blocks. I would spend the next few hours recouping, as the exhaustion made it impossible to do much else. My body constantly reminded me of its limitations, which could have become discouraging over time. However, I began to treat it like a child that needed love and nurturing. I was being tested in the area of caring for the body I had ignored for years, and I was determined to pass with flying colours. Worn out, it simply needed a chance to catch up and to be treated with an attitude of kindness.

At the beginning of chemo, I was told that if my treatment lasted seven months, my recovery would be about the same. I heard this, but never entertained it as truth until I experienced it. Assessing the fallout, I realized that the cells needed to rebuild, and the muscles and bones needed time to gather strength. Once I understood a bit more about what was happening in my body (and my soul), it made it easier to know what to leave at the cross. After prayerfully working through the emotions and trauma, I started to feel like my old self again—no more limbo.

I was encouraged to see the muscles respond fairly quickly to the gentle regime. Many days on the rowing machine or bicycle I would see myself as an athlete in training. (When you are not going anywhere, you have lots of time for prayer and reflection!) As I pushed the extra mile or two, I would hold onto the hope of a body that would be whole again. I was not looking to compete in the Olympics but simply wanted to restore my tired, wounded temple.

Patience is a vital element in the creation of any great work, but is not easily acquired. Throughout this gradual process of rebuilding my body, the Lord graciously compared it to the creation of a lovely pearl.

> Again, the kingdom of heaven is like a merchant seeking beautiful pearls, who, when he had found one pearl of great price, went and sold all that he had and bought it (Matthew 13:45–46 NKJV®).

I have always been fascinated with the natural creation of a pearl. An oyster is such an unlikely vessel for such a beautiful gem, as from the outside they are really quite ugly—uneven shells in mute colours of grey, often covered with green algae.

As a child I remember finding one and trying with all my strength to force it open, hoping to find a pearl inside. To my chagrin I made quite a mess and was dismayed to discover that it contained no buried treasure. I had heard that the oyster only produced a pearl if it had a small stone or grain of sand in its centre, so my friend suggested we replace the open shell into the sandy beach with the oyster face down and return the following week to claim our pearl. We forgot about it until a few weeks later when we were absentmindedly walking along the same stretch of beach and suddenly remembered the oyster. We ran to dig it out, but it was nowhere to be found. In a quandary we concluded that someone must have stumbled upon our precious gem and stolen it. I am sure that God laughed at this child-like faith as we believed and hoped for something valuable to be created quickly and easily.

I continue to make Him laugh as I often ask Him to bless my agenda and then cannot understand why something has not happened according to my timeframe. I am a product of this current generation that desires everything quickly. With all the timesaving inventions and comforts we have at our disposal, we should have so much more time on our hands! Many times throughout my treatment I would grow restless, satisfied with the lessons I had learned and eager just to have the whole ordeal finished. In the midst of sheer exhaustion and repeated trips to the cross, my heart would question, "Is this *really* necessary?" Without hesitation, the answer came to me from His Holy Word—*endurance and patience assure us of our inheritance.*

> Being strengthened with all power according to his glorious might so that you may have great endurance and patience, and joyfully giving thanks to the Father, who has qualified you to share in the inheritance of the saints in the kingdom of light (Colossians 1:11–12).
>
> We do not want you to become lazy, but to imitate those who through faith and patience inherit what has been promised (Hebrews 6:12).

The depth of our character governs the level of battles we are qualified to engage in. Only during times of trial and weakness is our true character exposed. Whether it is our physical bodies or mental fatigue, our lack of strength makes it impossible to keep up our facade, and the ugly truth is revealed. The Lord then gently removes the rough edges to create a beautiful jewel. The process of producing a pearl can actually take three to five years, which certainly would be a test of endurance and patience if I was an oyster.

As I emerged from the valley of darkness, I was grateful that the Lord was leading the way and was in charge of the schedule. I would be so disappointed to think I had given up too early and missed out on all that He had planned for my future. If I had not allowed Him to complete the extent of sanctification within me that He had achieved, I would not be equipped to step into the fullness of my destiny. The bonus was that I discovered the depth of the love He has for me throughout the process of major "heart" surgery.

With the trauma behind me, peace once again returned to my soul. With a grateful heart I entered our church sanctuary one Sunday morning, lifting my hands in praise and worship. My attention was drawn to a banner that hangs on the wall behind the piano. On a background of deep fiery shades of reds and yellow it displays the words from 1 Corinthians 13 on love. Pondering each quality of love, it became a *rhema* word, or living word, that ignited a greater passion in my heart for Jesus. I recalled the patience He had had for me; His kindness towards me as He lovingly revealed the truth; the protection of His hand upon me at every moment. He was never angry or rude, but rather instilled within me hope and perseverance and proved that love never fails. Through every trial, every test, every tear, every sorrow, every waking moment, and even those when I was asleep, He was as close as my breath.

> He has taken me to the banquet hall, and his banner
> over me is love (Song of Songs 2:4).

All year I had been standing beneath His magnificent banner of love as my beloved worked to create a pearl of great price.

chapter twenty

Hope

We have this hope as an anchor for the soul, firm and secure.
HEBREWS 6:19

H aving navigated through the storm, I had finally made it to a safe harbour and was ready to drop anchor for a time of rest and restoration. The worst was now behind me and I was beginning to find my bearings once again.

The book of Hebrews tells us that hope is like an anchor for our soul, "firm and secure." As I reflected on the many times that I had anchored a boat, I began to grasp how our level of faith influences the depth of our hope.

Some sailors make anchoring a boat look easy, but it isn't: many factors are involved in achieving a good hold. The weight of the anchor must be correct for the size of the vessel, the rope must be strong, and the shackles and fittings secure. Before anchoring, it is important to check the charts to determine the depth and type of ocean floor and the height of the tides. Calculating the correct amount of line to let out with the anchor is another important step so that the boat does not end up "short," or drift too close to shore. It can take many attempts before getting what you believe is a good hold . . . and then you wait. Boaters with little experience often do not get much sleep the first few nights until they become familiar with the process and develop a confidence in their anchor and their ability to achieve a good set. So just as preparation results in a restful night at anchor, it also plays a big part in establishing hope and faith within our soul.

> Consequently, faith comes from hearing the message, and the message is heard through the word of Christ (Romans 10:17).

I see now that every teaching, every sermon, and every chapter and verse that I have read over the years have planted within me a foundation of faith, making room for hope to bloom.

> For everything that was written in the past was written to teach us, so that through endurance and the encouragement of the Scriptures we might have hope (Romans 15:4).

A quiet harbour is a welcome respite from turbulent seas, but the holding power of an anchor is only really tested in a storm—just so with our hope and faith. When we stand on the bow of a boat looking down into the water, we do not *see* the anchor, but we nevertheless have faith that it will hold when the wind and rain come.

> Consider it pure joy, my brothers, whenever you face trials of many kinds, because you know that the testing of your faith develops perseverance (James 1:2—3).

Throughout the period of waiting out the storm, I had the opportunity to reflect on life and death. Seldom have I witnessed such a contrast between the two extremes. While I was writing this book, I experienced a setback when my mum became ill. My focus turned towards spending time with her and helping Dad find out why her health was failing.

Mum always had the exuberance and strength of a thirty-year-old, her enthusiasm inevitably touching those around her and leaving them with either an added spring in their step or completely exhausted! When she developed a blood clot in her leg, in true form, she did not let it hold her back but continued to hobble around in the garden, intent on pulling out one more weed. As the pain increased and the swelling in her leg restricted her mobility even more, it was clear that her body wanted her to slow down, but she was not very accommodating.

When the swelling did not respond to medication, the doctor ordered more tests. The results were devastating: a cancerous tumour in her liver. An accurate diagnosis at this point was impossible as this tumour was secondary to one they believed to be growing in her gall bladder. With the cancer too advanced to treat, a biopsy was not recommended and surgery was not an option. Following consultations with an array of doctors and specialists she was told that she had between six and twelve months to live.

Nothing prepares you for this kind of diagnosis, and again our family found itself in unfamiliar territory. Suffering from declining strength and the side effects of her prescriptions, Mum made several trips to the emergency room. Thankfully, one doctor was brave enough to give us the straight truth—Mum had less than two months to live.

As it turned out, Mum died five weeks after her first diagnosis. Our lives were turned completely upside down as Lesley, Dad, and I began to process all that had happened in two short months. This was the first time that I had had to deal with this level of grief and I was unprepared for all that death takes with it.

When someone you dearly love passes away, many things within you die with them. Plans you had for your future with that person cease and any questions will remain unanswered. What surprised me the most was that many hopes in my heart died with Mum—hopes that I was unaware of; hopes of dreams yet to be realized and events I would like to have shared with her. With so much to do in the first few weeks after her death, I had little time to reflect. My natural instinct was to go into survival mode. I have come to respect this as a built-in defence mechanism that protected me until I could get over the shock of having lost my mum.

Taking one day at a time was the most I could do as I struggled to find my way. I used what strength I had to hold my dad up as he too was trying to process the shock of Mum's passing. In consoling him I tended to guard my heart and ignore my own emotions. Only in the months following was I brave enough to emotionally unpack all that I had allow to remain dormant.

As this book sat on the shelf, unfinished, for nearly a year, so much more was going on within my soul. My testimony of hope, courage, and strength was being tested in away that I had not expected.

With my body still weak from the chemotherapy, I was again being thrown into the ring to face two more giants. The enemies of Death and Destruction were once again at my heels, reminding me of their presence only months after I had defeated them in my own life. My instinct was to run and hide away from the world, as I just could not endure anymore. I was weary and lacked the confidence to proceed. Pondering the magnitude of this battlefield, the Lord reminded me of the truth about war. Undoubtedly there would be casualties, but I must remember the victories that have been won. Not all will win their battles against cancer, but my hope is in knowing that we will one day be reunited in heaven.

Through little effort of my own, the qualities that He had laid as a foundation within me began to spring up. I simply declared my utter dependence upon Him, daily professing my willingness to yield to His ways and His purposes and the life within me gave me strength and purpose to carry on.

> I can do everything through him who gives me strength. (Philippians 4:13).

Knowing that someone I loved had been promoted to glory made me want to run that much farther and faster to defeat the enemy called Death. Sometimes I felt like an athlete who moans and complains when the coach keeps pushing her to go faster or higher. If I had to compete based on my own understanding and assessment, I would probably never have stepped up to the starting block.

How ironic that Mum had been sitting on the sidelines watching me bravely tackle breast cancer while cancer was quietly working through the organs in her body. As I was developing my arsenal of hope and strength, she was silently being overtaken by death. In a sense, I felt a bittersweet victory of triumph as I stood on the podium. A solemn silence remembered the life of one lost to cancer even as another soul survived.

> Let us throw off everything that hinders and the sin that
> so easily entangles, and let us run with perseverance
> the race marked out for us (Hebrews 12:1).

This has been a reminder to me of the battle we face every day. We live in a fallen world and do our best to run the race with perseverance, leaning on wisdom to supply a strategy for success. We face obstacles and need strength to endure. Hope is the fuel that keeps us moving, and courage gives us the confidence and boldness to overcome. Each of these traits are valuable qualities that are not easily acquired.

I know with certainty that Mum's spirit is in the arms of our beloved Jesus, as she believed in the cross and Jesus' sacrifice for her. Although she has left this earth, I am confident I will see her again at the greatest family reunion of all time.

> A faith and knowledge resting on the hope of eternal
> life, which God, who does not lie, promised before the
> beginning of time (Titus 1:2).

Peter's first epistle (1:4) talks about the inheritance that awaits us in heaven, an inheritance that cannot perish, spoil, or fade. Our citizenship is in heaven, so I see Mum as having passed on to a place that has been prepared for her, receiving an inheritance that was promised. Now that someone I love is there, heaven is so much closer to me and I have great joy in my heart when I imagine her looking out of heaven's windows. Jesus often reminds me of her closeness as I carry on her legacy.

Often it is only when we have a brush with death that we are moved to consider what we are put on this earth to do. When Death and Destruction hand us a blow, the pain can ignite a passion for life that cannot be suppressed.

Somewhere along the road of my battle, the seed of justice was planted within me to see cancer defeated. The mortality rate for this disease is alarming. According to the Canadian Cancer Society, in 2006, the same year as my battle took place, 153,100 *new* cases of cancer were diagnosed in Canada, with 46 percent of the victims dying. That's more than thirteen hundred people dying of cancer every week, just in Canada.

Another staggering statistic is the tally of potential "lost" years by those who prematurely die from cancer. Assuming that men and women have a life expectancy in their seventies, the number of lost years is arrived at by subtracting the age of their premature deaths from the normal life span. In 2002 in Canada, the total lost years due to cancer was more than three million! (Just as a rough calculation, if you take an average of forty-five lost years for one person and multiply it by the cancer deaths of approximately seventy thousand in a year, it totals more than three million.) Upon grasping this, I immediately began to weep as I realized how many years of destiny had been robbed by the destroyer, Satan. Consider how much could be accomplished in three million life years. For every year of destiny that has been stolen, what plans did the Lord have for those precious lives?

> Your enemy the devil prowls around like a roaring
> lion looking for someone to devour (1 Peter 5:8).

In each generation there has been a hardening of hearts towards the voice of God. Most of us (including me) accept the rising numbers of deaths due to cancer until we are personally touched by it. Millions of dollars go into the research of cancer, and thankfully this has saved many lives, including my own. I think however, that we need to reposition ourselves from a place of *defence*, to one of attack and *offence*. As long as we continue to tolerate the enemy's scheme to destroy multitudes with this disease, he will use it as a weapon against us.

The passion that burns within me today is to see people find their hope, strength, and courage at the source, Jesus. I have lived the truth that as you pursue Him, you will find Him. It is His breath that infuses life and hope into hearts that desire to know Him. His word says to seek first the kingdom of God and His righteousness. (Matthew 6:33) When we lay hold of His kingdom, we find wisdom and power to defeat every assault from the enemy. In His strength we can make it through any storm and the Lord will be the lighthouse that safely guides us into quiet, protected waters.

chapter twenty-one

Passing Under the Rainbow

The desert and the parched land will be glad; the wilderness
will rejoice and blossom. Like the crocus, it will burst
into bloom; it will rejoice greatly and shout for joy.
ISAIAH 35:1–2

The book of Ecclesiastes describes the many "seasons for every activity under heaven." The promise is that for every trial there is a triumph and for every sorrow a time to rejoice. Having faced death and endured grief, the time of mourning has come to an end. It is a new day with countless opportunities peeking over the horizon, ushered in by the bright Morning Star.

My heart is filled with gratitude that it is beyond words. Nobody could have carried the weight of my burdens as the Lord did through every stage of this journey through breast cancer. He directed me to be strong and courageous for He was with me. He tenderly spoke words of truth to set me free and surrounded me with comfort when words escaped my lips. He taught me when to speak and when to listen; when to war and when to stand. Through every fear, every battle, and every tear, He was there. With every sharp edge that He cut away, light came forth from darkness, producing a beautiful diamond from a simple hunk of coal.

I have reached a depth of love for Him that moves me to tears—a natural response to the touch of His gentle hand upon my heart. In the quietness of suffering I grew to understand the meaning of His declaration, "Be still and know that I am God." The many ways of God are too lofty to comprehend, and yet He unlocked my understanding to see a lovely ray of His beauty shine upon my life.

The many "coincidences" that occurred during this entire experience make it nearly impossible for anyone to argue that God does not exist. He is a God who hears, speaks, and feels, and whose creativity paves the way for endless possibilities. We will never comprehend all the facets and multiple dimensions of God until we reach heaven, but He does give us an opportunity to continually reach higher and know more of His magnificent mysteries.

I watched Him weave a canvas together under one banner called love, expressed through qualities that are unique to His women. In the Bible, the breast is a symbol of contentment and blessing. In an effort to help me understand the mystery of breast cancer, He revealed the bitterness towards mothers that existed in my family for at least three generations. As I dealt with this sin by nailing it to the cross, the Lord brought healing and restoration, aligning me to receive blessing. I was thankful that the relationship with my own mother had an opportunity to be healed before it was too late.

Many revelations were illustrated through scenarios relating to women and to motherhood. If you recall, the first message I heard in my heart regarding my diagnosis came on the evening I spoke to our woman's group. Following that, a Mother's Day gift exposed my need to fast and pray—a message I received through my own mother. The vision regarding my body as the child who was ignored was displayed through a picture of a mother sitting around the table with three little girls. Even the Lord's confirmation of treatment was revealed through "spilled milk."

Leading up to Christmas, the Lord continued to encourage and bless me through my slow transition to recovery. He confirmed that I was a Sarah to this generation, as many friends and strangers mistakenly called me Sarah. Laughter was hard to contain when someone with a wrong number called, asking for Sarah Crawford. On Christmas Eve I was delighted to receive a gift from a neighbour I had not seen in months. For no apparent reason, she gave me a lovely collector's plate with a picture of a young girl named Sarah, who, with wide eyes, stared at a flickering candle that caused the decorative angels to dance around it. Another reminder that His angels are winds, and I, His servant, am a flame of fire. This is the faithfulness of God and the love of a Father who wants us to be whole again.

> Every good and perfect gift is from above, coming down from the Father of the heavenly lights, who does not change like shifting shadows (James 1:17).

What I marvel at the most is how the Lord opens up our heart to know Him on such an intimate level. It is in the details that we can be assured of His watchful eye upon us, confident that He continues the deep work within us.

A few months after my mum's passing, I stumbled upon a large box in which she used to store Christmas gifts that she gathered throughout the year. With some hesitation, I took a deep breath and reached in to pull out the items she had hand-picked. Buried beneath the assorted boxes, I discovered a soft package carefully wrapped in plastic to keep it from getting dusty. Sitting alone on the wooden boards of the attic, I felt that all of heaven was watching and waiting to see my reaction.

Removing the tissue revealed a beautiful handmade quilt for a baby's crib. One side of the quilt was made up of many small squares, all perfectly matched and sewn together—blue, green, pink, yellow, and purple. The tiny pieces of fabric were adorned with pictures of toys, clowns, and trains, all with a soft fleece backing patterned with rainbows. Mum had an eye for beauty and quality in things that others would not see. As I embraced the quilt, the softness of the fleece caressed my face and I felt the pleasure she must have experienced when she spotted this precious gift. Never being a grandmother was a great sadness for her. This moment brought me closer to her heart as we walked through a similar disappointment; I felt as though cords of our hearts were joined together with each thread of the fabric—the lid of a hope chest thrown open to reveal dreams that had been locked away.

Finding this quilt proved to be a tipping point for complete healing in my relationship with my mother. The walls around her heart had often made it hard for us to connect, and in God's wisdom this treasure unlocked chambers shrouded in darkness. It allowed me to embrace the person behind all of her hurts and appreciate the truth that it was the loving prayers of a mother that had turned my heart towards Jesus many years ago.

Throughout my treatments I shared many profound insights with Mum. These were precious times when we rejoiced in the goodness of the Lord. Now that she is in glory, I believe she is cheering me on. Mum was tired—she had run her race and was ready to spend eternity with the Jesus she loves. She now has a front row seat and in typical form, is probably shouting the loudest, now that her sorrows have turned into dancing.

In the small village of Deep Cove, we see many rainbows in the spring. Carrying on in the tradition of my mum, whenever I see one I run to the window to take in the wonder of God's beauty, a confirmation that He is a God who keeps His promises. I am not sure why we are so fascinated with finding each end of the rainbow—perhaps we hope to glimpse something more. Dark clouds are always present on one side of any rainbow, but they appear to be drawn back like a curtain as the colours reveal fresh hope in the brightness of the sun. What a spectacular display from the God who loves us!

Leaning on the arm of my beloved Jesus, I emerge from under the dark clouds of the storm with renewed hope. I do not know what my future holds, but I trust in the One who is holding my hand. He has healed me and blessed me beyond anything I could ask or imagine. I have cried tears of sorrow and grief, walked through fears, and found answers for every honest question of my heart. I have experienced His power and been showered in grace. He has never taken His eyes off me and has lovingly guided me past every obstacle. With patience

He has fashioned me into a warrior who has the ability to overcome every force of evil that would rise against me. John 16:11 tells us, "The prince of this world now stands condemned," which is one of the greatest truths we can embrace as we face every battle. Infusing me with His strength, He created a woman of courage and valour who has faith to believe the victory has been won. Fires of hope burn within my heart, as I behold the glorious face of my beloved Jesus. He has infiltrated every cell of my being with His unfailing love that conquers all.

In the cold of winter, the crocus finds courage to peek through the blanket of snow, reaching to find the light. As spring bursts forth from the trees, I feel the warmth of the sun upon my own face. The fullness of God's love is breathing new life and hope into this woman who is emerging from under the rainbow, stepping over the threshold into an exciting destiny.

It Ends Here.

appendix A

Declarations of Truth

The word of God is powerful and effective. Even when Jesus was tempted by the enemy, He responded with "It is written . . ." As we find ourselves reaching out to the Lord, we too can see the power of God at work through our simple prayers of faith. The following prayers have been crafted from verses in the Bible—many in a single prayer. A comprehensive concordance is a good resource if you wish to locate the specific passage.

Throughout the pages of my story, I have recounted the goodness and faithfulness of God as He led me through the valley of the shadow of death. As you begin your journey, take hold of His hand and ask that He take you to a deeper level of love. The word of God proclaims that "if God be for us, who can be against us?" This is a great reminder that although the Lord allows these trials, He is on your side. He knows your struggles and hears the cry of your heart.

Focus on the power of the Lord and His greatness, not on the schemes of the enemy. Jesus is the King of all kings, and Lord of all lords. He is the Lion of the Tribe of Judah who roars over His beloved children.

My prayer is that you will find hope with every one of these prayers and that your faith will be strengthened and your spirit stirred with every proclamation of truth. I pray that the Lord will give you a spirit of wisdom and revelation so that you may know him better. I pray that the eyes of your heart may be enlightened in order that you may know the hope to which he has called you, the riches of his glorious inheritance in the saints, and his incomparably great power for us who believe. That power is like the working of his mighty strength. (Ephesians 1:17—19)

Getting started.

Whenever you pray, it is important to have a place where you can sit quietly, without noise or distraction. If you have small children this can be challenging, but do your best to set aside a place and time that is just for you and God. Begin by thanking the Lord for every blessing in your life and singing a couple of choruses of praise and worship. This allows the cares of the world to slip away as your mind and heart focus on the Lord.

Before praying the following prayers, try to see things from a heavenly perspective. Remember, we are seated with God in heavenly places! Begin with how the Lord sees *you*—the child that He loves. I have always felt that the best way to quiet my soul is to close my eyes and picture the cross. I mediate on all that it means and the love that is represented by Jesus' willingness to take all my sin upon Himself.

Thank you, Lord for the cross. Thank you for all that it represents. Thank you that it was the perfect, agape love from heaven that caused you to endure the pain and suffering. Thank you for taking my place. Thank you, Lord that you said, "It is finished," and that every sin, every illness, and every ailment can be nailed to the cross. It is finished.

Lord, I ask that you would open up the eyes and ears of my spirit to see and hear you clearly. I long to know you more. I ask that you would give me Godly wisdom and understanding.

Confessing your sins.

The word of God asks, "Who may ascend the mountain of the Lord? Those with clean hands and a pure heart." The condition of our heart is important if we expect to hear clearly from heaven and if we want our prayers to be heard.

Lord, I know that I am a sinner saved by your grace and your love. Thank you that for every sin, you offer forgiveness. Just as you taught the disciples to pray, I ask that you would forgive my sins. **(Wait in silence to see if the Lord reminds you of any specific areas you need to deal with.)** *Forgive me Lord.*

<u>Giving it back to God.</u>
When you have been diagnosed with cancer, it is understandable that you have many emotions to sort through, as your soul has just been handed a blow. What is most important right now is honesty. Be honest with yourself and honest with God. This is where the deepest freedom and healing will come from throughout the entire journey. You may be angry with God. If so, then admit it and have a heart to heart talk with Him. Maybe it is a loved one that has been diagnosed with cancer and you feel frustrated. Frustration is a sign of wanting to control things that are beyond your control, so maybe it is time to offer it all up to the Lord.

Lord, I don't understand why you are allowing these things to happen in my life **(or in _____'s life)** *right now. But, I believe that your plans are to prosper me and not to harm me. I believe that you want to give me hope and a future. Revive my hope to believe in a brighter tomorrow. I know that your ways are higher than my ways; your thoughts are higher than my thoughts. I fully surrender my life to you. I pray that you would have your way with me, and that you would transform me into the woman (man) of God that you always meant for me to be. Lord, I trust in you and believe that your promises are true. I love you and know that the love you have for me is beyond anything I have ever known in this world. Help me to know the depth of your love for me.*

Strength, Favour and Peace.

Lord, give me strength to endure all that comes my way. I ask for discernment to know when you are speaking to me, and wisdom to do all that you ask and direct.

Lord, I ask that your favour and grace would rest upon me. For every procedure I undergo, for every treatment I endure, I know that you have hand-picked the doctors and nurses that will care for me. I ask that you would give them Godly wisdom on how best to treat me. I ask for skill and precision. I ask for only the number of treatments that you have ordained—no more, no less. I am believing for a complete healing in every part of me; my body, my soul, and my spirit.

Your peace that passes all understanding will rest upon me day and night. You, the God that neither slumbers nor sleeps, will watch over me at all times. You will dispatch your angels on my behalf. They will fight in the unseen battle and I proclaim the victory of Jesus over cancer. My body will be healed. All will be well with my soul as damaged emotions will be healed, strongholds of the mind will be broken, and I choose to yield to the ways of the Lord, God Almighty, the One who was and is, and is to come.

Declaration of Victory!

Lord, your word says that you will give back all that the locusts have eaten. For everything that the enemy has stolen, I ask for a sevenfold return. Whether it be finances, resources, time, relationships or joy; restore all that has been taken from me. I believe that you work all things together for good. I believe that good will come out of this experience. I will be changed and I will grow in character and strength. I will emerge with courage, with hope, and with strength. People will be touched and blessed and changed by what you are doing in me. The voice of the enemy will be silenced and the mocker will speak no more. Every false god will bow their knee to the powerful name of Jesus. I will walk in victory!

A cleansing prayer. There's power in the blood of Jesus!
Lord, I thank you for the precious blood of Jesus that took away the
sins of the world. I thank you that one drop of the blood of Jesus is
enough to drive out the enemy. I ask you to cleanse every part of this
room and everything in it. Thank you that you are not confined by
our limits of time. I ask that you would walk through the history of
this house (hospital room, etc.) cleansing it from all defilements
and deposits of evil. Lord, drive out any spirits of the enemy that
reside here. I declare this room to be holy ground, and that your
purposes will prevail. Cleanse every pair of hands that will touch
me. I bind them to your perfect will. I bind up the work of the enemy
in bringing delay or distractions of any kind, and declare that the
favour of the Lord rests upon me. I declare the victory of Calvary
over all that will be done in my life today. Hallelujah!

A prayer of comfort.
Lord, I thank you for your Holy Spirit who is our counsellor and
guide; our source of comfort. I ask that you would surround me on
every side, reminding me of your love. Drive away my fears and
wipe away my tears. Help me to lean on you. Stir up the hope that
is within me. Infuse me with your strength. I thank you that you
are with me, and that you know all that I am thinking and feeling.
Thank you that your word says you gather the lambs in your arms
and carry them close to your heart. Let me hear your tender whisper
that says, "This is the way, walk ye in it." I thank you, Lord, that you
rejoice over me with singing.

Thank you Lord that your word says you have redeemed me; you
have called me by name. Thank you that as I pass through the
waters, you will be with me; when I pass through the rivers, they
will not sweep over me; when I walk through the fire, I will not be
burned, the flames will not set me ablaze. Thank you that you have
me in the palm of your hand, and nothing can separate me from
your love.

Prayers of repentance.

Repentance means that you want to turn from sin and no longer give it room in your life. An important key to healing is to remember that generations before us may have opened the door to sin that could still have an effect on us today. As I waited on the Lord, He revealed that I needed to repent for many generations that harboured bitterness towards mothers. Taking time to wait is vital to see what He shows you about your own sins or those of previous generations. Many believers offer prayers to the Lord, but never wait to hear His response. The word of God says that the Lord's *kindness* leads us to repentance. If you feel like you are receiving a harsh rebuke, then this is the voice of the enemy bringing condemnation. If however, you feel a sincere sadness when you are reminded of a time in history or shown a picture, this is the Lord's kind, gentle way of revealing a truth to you. If you do not fully understand what He is showing you, ask questions and He will be faithful to give you direction. When the complete story is revealed, you will know with certainty what He is asking you to nail to the cross.

The simple steps to freedom are to forgive those involved for their part in the hurt or sin and ask the Lord to forgive you for your part in it. If you are having a hard time forgiving them, continue with prayers of blessing over them. Remember to forgive yourself. Forgiveness tends to break up the logjams. Finally, confess your willingness to change and ask for healing. It is as simple as that!

Example 1: *The generational sin of bitterness towards mothers.*
Lord, thank you for revealing the presence of this bitter root within me and within my family. I ask for forgiveness and stand in the gap to repent on behalf of every generation before me that also opened the door to this sin. I ask that you would forgive us for allowing bitterness to enter our hearts that was directed towards our mothers. I thank you Lord that you ordained, before the foundation of the earth, who my mother would be. I thank you that there are blessings that have come through her generational line. I thank you for the life of my mother. I realize that nobody is given an

instruction manual when we come forth from the womb, and I know my mother did the best job she knew how. I forgive her for every curse word she thought or spoke over me or to me. I ask that you would forgive me for every curse word I thought or spoke over her or to her. I choose to forgive her and to forgive myself. I repent for this sin and receive your forgiveness. I pull out every root of bitterness that grew from my actions and nail it to the cross. I break off every last bit of entanglement with this bitterness from the place of its origin. I receive the blood of Jesus to wash me clean of all sin. Heal my wounded heart and the heart of my mother. Lord, bind us together with chords of love, redeeming all that has been lost in our relationship.

Example 2: The vision the Lord showed me about having abused my body. Lord, I ask that you would reveal any sin that would block a complete healing. **(Wait on the Lord's response.)**

Thank you for showing me how I have silenced the voice of my body and never paid attention to it. I ask that you would forgive me for abusing this body. Your word says that my body is the temple of the Holy Spirit, and I have defiled it in so many ways. I ask that you would forgive me for hating the appearance of this body. I realize that I have not valued the gift you have given me. Forgive me for vanity. Forgive me for not appreciating that I am created in the image of your Son Jesus and that each of your children is precious to you. I thank you that you look upon the heart, and that judgments of outer appearances are of the world. Forgive me for every shred of self-hatred. I also forgive myself for my mistakes and for not realizing what you have given me. Thank you for this body. I ask that you would open my ears to hear the voice of this body, and I ask for Godly wisdom to make good choices and properly care for it. Lord, I repent for all these sins and nail them to the cross. I receive your forgiveness and believe that this body will be blessed by you. I ask that you would heal this body from the top of my head to the soles of my feet.

Facing the enemy head on.

Lord, I thank you that your promise is that you will never leave nor forsake me. I thank you that you are the One who helped David slay Goliath, simply with a stone and a slingshot. Thank you for arming me with your word that is a double-edged sword. As I face the giant of cancer, give me the courage to acknowledge that my name is on his lips. As I look him square in the face, I thank you that you surround me on every side and the enemy knows that I am hidden in you. Thank you for your word that says that you are a strong tower, that as I run into you, I am safe. Thank you that your word says that as I dwell in the shelter of the Most High God, I will rest in the shadow of the Almighty. Thank you that you save me from the fowler's snare and from deadly pestilence. Thank you that I will find refuge under your wings. I will not fear the terror of night nor the arrow that flies by day, nor the pestilence that stalks in the darkness, nor the plague that destroys at midday. Thank you that no weapon formed against me shall prosper. Lord, as I look into the face of cancer, I stand protected by the blood of Jesus. I rebuke every spirit of cancer and every spirit of infirmity. In the mighty name of Jesus I command that every spirit of darkness that has come against me go to the place of its demise at the foot of the cross. With the sword of the Lord in my hand, I cut off every entanglement with the spirits of darkness and declare that I am a child of the Most High God. I am my beloved's and He is mine. I crush the head of the enemy and he is now under my feet. Thank you Lord!

A prayer of release from trauma.

Lord, thank you for carrying me through the battle. Thank you that you have breathed life back into me. I ask that you would release me from every bit of trauma that came upon me. I forgive every technician, every doctor, and every nurse that was used by the enemy to inflict pain or trauma through their words or actions. I know that they worked to save my life. I release them to you Lord and ask that you would bless them. I thank you that you have never left me. Thank you that you were on the battlefield with me, directing and leading me to victory. I ask now that by the power of the name of Jesus you would remove every residue of trauma and every entanglement. Lord, apply your healing balm of Gilead to the places that caused me to become withdrawn or afraid. I release every fear, every sting of the pain and leave it at the foot of the cross. Let the hope of my destiny be renewed. Allow the joy that is set before me to soak into every fibre of my being. Thank you precious Jesus for your love that washes over me.

A prayer for healing.
Lord, thank you that you are the God who heals us. Thank you for revelation that will unlock the door to healing. Thank you that your word says that you forgive all my sins and heal all my diseases. Thank you that you send forth your word to rescue me from the pit and from destruction. I shall not die, but LIVE! I will live every last day that you ordained for me on this earth. I will run the race with perseverance and lay hold of all that you laid hold of for me.

Thank you Lord that you not only heal my body but also my broken heart, and that you take all my sorrows. You bind up my wounds and bring healing to every part of my innermost being. Your words are truth. I will hold them in my heart, for they are the wellspring of life. Your word says that by your stripes I am healed, and I believe it as truth. Your word says that a prayer offered in faith will make a sick person well.

A prayer for courage.
Lord, I thank you for so many testimonies in your word of men and women who struggled to find courage, but truth prevailed and they overcame their fears. I thank you for Joshua of old who many times needed to be encouraged and reminded of your presence. Just as you did for him, I ask that you would make me strong and courageous. I believe that you are with me and you will give me strength. Give me faith in the place of fear. Stir my faith to hope and believe for all the good that is yet to come in my life. Give me faith to believe that I

will make it through this storm. Allow me to see what is beyond this horizon and into my future. Restore the vision of why you called me to be alive on the earth for this time in history. With your mighty winds, blow upon the flame and purposes in my heart. Remind me of the passions you placed within me. Lift me up above the darkness of today and into the glorious light of tomorrow. Remove me from the chords of death and draw me into the light of life. Your word says that as I walk through the valley of the shadow of death I will fear no evil for you are with me. Lord, make this a reality to me. Show me your power, and manifest it through this willing vessel. I know the truth of what you can accomplish through one willing soul. Even Moses doubted his ability, yet we know of his great exploits, because you are a mighty God. You are the Alpha and Omega, the Beginning and the End. You are outside of time as eternity is in your hands. Heaven is your throne and the earth is your footstool. I praise you Lord for the victory that is ours. I thank you that your word says that everyone born of God overcomes the world!

I will be strong and courageous because the Lord, my God is with me. He promises to never leave nor forsake me. I put my hope in the Lord.

A prayer for spiritual armour.
Lord, thank you for the blood of Jesus that covers and protects me. I put on the full armour of God: The belt of truth to gird my loins; to envelope every part of my core being. I am protected and will stand firm on your truth. I put on the breastplate of righteousness to protect my heart. I pray I will always respond with the goodness and righteousness of God against every fiery dart of the enemy that comes my way. I place upon my head the helmet of salvation and hope that will infuse hope into every thought pattern in my mind. I take every thought captive and will declare the goodness and blessing and hope of the Lord in every situation. I place upon my feet, the shoes of the gospel of peace. Your word is a lamp to my feet and a light for my path. I pray your peace will go before me and

surround me on every side. I lift up my shield of faith. Let faith arise to deflect every flaming arrow of the enemy, to silence the voice of the tormentors, and to release a spirit of hope in the place of fear. Lord, I thank you for the sword of the spirit that you have placed in my hand. I thank you that as I wield this sword, the enemy will be taken out at the knees. I thank you that you have placed the enemy under my feet! Let God arise and His enemies be scattered. Thank you that the enemy will be defeated before my very eyes and he shall flee in every direction.

And finally, my prayer for you:
I pray that out of the glorious riches of the Lord, He will strengthen you with power through His Spirit in your inner being, so that Christ may dwell in your hearts through faith. I pray that you, being rooted and established in love, may have the power, together with all the saints, to grasp how wide and long and high and deep is the love of Christ, and to know this love that surpasses knowledge—that you may be filled to the measure of all the fullness of God (Ephesians 3:16-19).

Lord, we ask all these things in the powerful name of Jesus and for your glory. AMEN!

appendix B

Practically Speaking

I compiled these points as some practical advice for patients, my "comrades".[9] I hope you will find them helpful, and that perhaps they will bring you a smile or two. God bless you and keep you as you fight this battle with hope, courage, and strength.

Before treatment begins
Develop a rapport with your oncologist and nurses.
Take an active role in your treatment early on by asking questions about anything that is unclear. The doctors and nurses cannot read your mind, so speak up! If you have concerns, ask them to clarify the facts so you can be confident of the process. Most will value your honesty and transparency, and it will help them give you the best care and attention possible.

Prepare some small meals in advance and put them in the freezer.
Single precooked portions of a variety of foods will help when you just do not know what your stomach can take. Good, healthy soups are a great idea. If you are not able to make them yourself, buy organic soups in small cartons that do not require refrigeration. Favourites of

---
9   These suggestions are not intended to replace any advice given to you by your doctor or other healthcare practitioners.

mine were butternut squash, chicken noodle, and (of course) Sandra's famous broccoli soup.

Stock the shelves!
Staples that I stashed in my pantry:
- ❑ saltine crackers
- ❑ granola bars
- ❑ plain digestive cookies
- ❑ ginger ale
- ❑ soups, such as butternut squash, broccoli, and chicken noodle
- ❑ assorted breads and crackers
- ❑ cheese (crackers and cheese were one of my favourites as a main course)
- ❑ snack pak sizes of chocolate pudding
- ❑ individual servings of apple sauce
- ❑ snack pak sizes of canned fruit
- ❑ trail mix with nuts and seeds—packed full of nutrients
- ❑ chocolate!

Preparation and paperwork.
It can be quite a task updating friends and family on your progress, so if possible, ask a close friend or family member to keep people updated on your behalf. Try to arrange to have your bills paid in advance or automatically, and tend to other paperwork as you won't feel like doing this once treatment starts. Clear your calendar so that you do not have any obligations to anyone other than yourself. Your focus must remain on the battle at hand!

During chemotherapy
Drink up!
Stay well hydrated before each blood test, as this simplifies the technicians' task in locating a vein. This also reduces the feeling of being a human pin cushion!

You won't be climbing Everest.
Although there will be days when you have very little strength, do your best to exercise. A walk around the block is better than nothing at all and will make your recovery easier.

Hair today, gone tomorrow.
Ladies, get friendly with your hairdresser. Before your hair starts to fall out, progressively get shorter haircuts, as it will help you to cope with eventual loss of hair. Have some fun with different hairstyles in the few weeks before you lose it all. I discovered that I actually preferred short hair! (An added bonus is that once you lose your hair, you also won't have to shave your legs for a few months!)

Top model material.
Ladies, learn different ways of tying a scarf so you can be creative with your head coverings. Practice when you have enough strength to keep your arms over your head. Sometimes I was willing to settle for a brown paper bag!

Pack a hospital goodie bag.
Find yourself a small, pretty, bag to use for your trips to the hospital on treatment day. Pack some crackers, cheese, music with headphones, reading material, and just in case . . . a barf bag for the car ride.

Got milk?
Some chemo drugs deplete your body's calcium, turning your muscles into mush. In the process of rebuilding muscle strength, calcium tablets are an essential supplement to avoid loss of bone density. If your body does not have enough calcium, it begins to steal it from your bones. This is why doctors usually suggest a bone density test immediately following your treatment as it gives them a benchmark for further tests as well as providing you with a clear picture of your progress.

Short and sweet.
If you are on a chemo drug that causes your fingernails and toenails to fall off, keep them clipped short. As they begin to lift off, they become tender and can easily get caught in clothing which is painful!

Smile!
One side effect of some chemo drugs is dry mouth, so understandably, bacteria and plaque can develop at a faster rate. I used an alcohol-free antibacterial rinse called Biotene.

Oops!
If you get diarrhea from the chemo drugs, act quickly. Whatever your strategy, whether an over-the-counter drug or specific foods that counteract diarrhea, remember that the drugs causing this side effect are strong, so fight back with full force. Don't become dehydrated and weak.

Oops again!
If you get constipated, see previous note. Don't wait; act immediately! I was in a lot of pain and started to develop a fever as my body was being poisoned through constipation.

I'm listening!
Listen to your body. As your blood levels fluctuate, you may have certain cravings. One day my desire for a strawberry papaya was so great that it gave me enough strength to get dressed and walk to the veggie stand across the street. Every slice of the fruit was like discovering an oasis in the middle of the desert. It contains many powerful enzymes that apparently my body needed at the time. On another occasion, my red cell count was bottoming out, giving me an overwhelming urge to eat a juicy hamburger—my body was looking for protein. As my body was being depleted of calcium, I craved ice cream and dairy products. Listen to the voice of your body!

There she goes!
When your red cell count drops, watch for signs of anaemia. Once I felt dizzy and became quite afraid as I did not know what was going on; only later did I realize I was bordering on anaemia. Looking back, I made a bad decision to wait it out alone instead of calling a friend to stay with me. Many times I came close to fainting, which could have been dangerous.

Dear diary.
After each treatment, keep a diary of how your body feels each day. List the side effects and any extra tablets you needed to take. Keeping accurate records of how you are responding to treatment will help the oncologist assist you.

Dear diary—me again.
Many cancer victims feel it is beneficial to keep a journal of all that is happening in their souls. Journaling can be a powerful tool in digging deeper and gaining revelation. I logged every scripture and encouraging word, as well as details of the emotional rollercoaster.

That's entertainment!
Many great resources are available to help you through the low times.

- ❑ Music — Have some music available for the chemo days when you need to build up your courage. Uplifting praise and worship songs helped me a lot.

- ❑ Sermons —Many free sermons can be found on the Internet. For a great selection, check out www.oneplace.com. This keeps your mind active when your body is weak. You may be amazed at how the Lord will bring some very timely messages to you.

❑ Movies on DVD. Stock up on your favourites.

❑ Bible on CD/mp3. A great investment. As I crawled into bed I often would put on a CD of the Psalms. This helped me sleep and the words went well beyond my conscious mind right into my spirit.

❑ Books on CD/mp3. When your eyes are tired, it is a great way to entertain yourself.

Pray without ceasing!
At times you will hardly be able to utter a word, so just do your best to focus on the closeness of the Lord. He knows your innermost thoughts and fears, so just talk to Him as you would your closest friend. He sticks closer than a brother!

Take communion for the pleasure, not the ceremony.
Take communion often. Searching your heart, confessing your sin, and reaffirming the love of the Lord for you in the sacrifice of Jesus is very powerful, building strength and faith.

Pow!
Use the word of God to keep the enemy back and to build up your spirit. Take scriptures and turn them into prayers. Proclamations of truth can change the atmosphere.

Post chemo/ radiation treatment
Cleanup.
Chemotherapy is poison, so be pro-active about detoxifying your body. Try different kinds of cleansings but remember, it takes more than a one-time, quick fix. Do not be discouraged if you do not see immediate results. Research different methods such as Epsom salt baths, and try the one that meets your needs. Check with your doctor before you embark upon any kind of cleansing or fast.

Get back up on the horse.
Getting your body back into shape will take some time. Start slowly and do not expect miracles in the first week. Exercise as much as you can manage and let your body rest when it needs to. "Gentle fit," or aqua-size classes are a great way to begin so that you do not put too much stress on your joints.

Everyone loves a great deal.
When signing up for a fitness program, check out your local community centre. Vancouver has a recreation commission with professionals who work with you to get you into shape. Meet with a counsellor to get some ideas for an exercise program suited to your needs. (Our local centre also gives you a price discount if you qualify as low income.) I was so encouraged when I began a fitness program, as I felt that a personal trainer was carrying on where the doctors left off. The compassion and consideration that the instructors and counsellors showed me helped immensely.

Basic training.
When you feel strong enough to do more strenuous exercises, promote yourself to the weight room. Start off with a few reps using light weights. "Muscle memory" ensures that as you begin to wake muscles up with exercise, they quickly respond.

Be patient and kind.
If you have not exercised for a period of time, it is natural to feel tired when you begin working out. Set a pace you are comfortable with and then gradually ramp up the workout times, always being careful not to overdo it. Be patient and kind to yourself!

Peach fuzz.
When your last chemo treatment is done, your hair will quickly begin to grow in again and will likely resemble peach fuzz. Use a gentle shampoo until the strands build strength. Avoid any harsh chemicals on your hair such as hair colouring.

One of the Three Stooges?
Often hair grows in curly, but typically this is only temporary, due to the fine texture of the strands, somewhat like baby's hair. It may go through a few phases of texture and colour before it gains strength and returns to normal.

Silky but slippery!
Some survivors recommend using satin pillowcases when the hair is growing back, as they are gentler on your hair as you sleep. I tried them but found that they were too slippery. My bald head would slip right off the pillow onto the mattress!

A happy head.
The vitamin biotin promotes healthy hair. If you take multi vitamins (a good idea), make sure that biotin is in the mix.

Remember those pearly whites.
After your treatments are over and you have regained some strength, visit your dentist as you may find that a lot of plaque has developed on your teeth. Ensure that your blood count is back to normal so your body can fight any germs that get into your blood stream from having your teeth cleaned. I declined a dental x-ray on my first visit, having just being exposed to a lot of radiation.

Her what?
Some studies say that eating red meat or drinking red wine can put one at risk for developing breast cancer. However, it seems that this only applies to people who have a "HER2 receptor." Ask if you have one or not. My understanding is that post-treatment hormone therapy will have no effect on anyone without this receptor. (If in doubt, check with your doctor. This point applied to my situation and is simply offered as a point to ponder.)

Friends for Life - Ideas for Friends and Caregivers

Y ou have a tough job because even the patient does not know what she[10] needs. She can change her mind from one moment to the next, so be patient. The best policy is to let her know that you are willing to help. Stay flexible, but be clear if you have limitations, such as only being available in the evenings. God bless you for your generous heart. You are more of a blessing than you know!

Dinner and a movie.
Offer to make her dinner in her home and ask what she would like to eat. Rent or buy a classic movie or a comedy. If she feels strong, consider going to a movie together.

Send cards and notes.
Cards: send all kinds and send them often. Get your kids to draw pictures or have your whole family sign a card. Funny cards are

---

[10] I have written these points from a woman's perspective, so thought it appropriate to refer to 'her', although I am sure that many men going through treatments would be blessed by the same ideas.

particularly uplifting instead of sorrowful cards reminding her of her troubles. Send a postcard of the city!

Send flowers (assuming that they don't have allergies!)
Fresh flowers and plants can be very uplifting for those long days of recovery on the sofa.

Buy scarves.
A hand picked scarf carries a lot of love. Stay away from materials that slip too easily, such as polyester. Pure cotton and some silks are great for the summer heat.

Bring gifts!
I always felt so spoiled when I received gifts for no apparent reason. Be creative—thoughtfulness always shines through.

Prepare meals.
Small, pre-cooked prepared meals are a great blessing. Even if her stomach is not up to it that night, she can stash it in the freezer until the time is right.

Chocolate.
Speaks for itself. Important enough to make it a separate item on the list!

Soups.
Gourmet or homemade soups can be a welcome change from canned soups. If you do not cook, stop by the local deli.

Show off your talents!
Everyone has a natural gift or talent, so use what has been given to you! If you have a gift of song, sing one. (Thank you Christine!) If you are an encourager, send notes often.

Be mindful of the patient when calling or visiting.
Depending upon the stage of treatment, your act of kindness may be at an inopportune time if she tires quickly. Check often to see if it is time to leave.

Park and drive.
Offer to take her on a drive or to sit in the park. If she's not up to it, offer again in a week. Let her know you are still thinking about her!

Coffee, tea, or me?
Invite her to go out for a coffee, tea, or ice cream. Getting out is always a welcome change of scenery, but on a bad day, think about showing up at her door with home delivery—but call first!

Board (or shall I say "bored") games.
She may become bored and welcome the opportunity to have someone drop by to play cards or a board game.

House cleaning.
Offer to do simple housekeeping tasks or laundry.

Grocery shopping.
A bag of groceries, including fresh fruit and veggies and wonderful breads, can be a real treat. Don't go overboard though, as too much can be overwhelming.

Prayer.
Never underestimate the power of prayer. Pray often and pray hard. You may be amazed at the mountains God will move for you!

Scripture Index

Chapter 1

Chapter 2

Chapter 3

Chapter 4

Chapter 10

Chapter 12

Chapter 11

Chapter 13

About the Author, Sandra Crawford

As a young girl, Sandra often sat on the floor of her mother's office, pecking out cheerful letters to "Mummy" on an old Underwood typewriter. Coming from a long line of letter writers, she soon demonstrated a natural ability to lift even the saddest heart with a simple note of encouragement or a heart-felt poem.

Growing up in an era of rapidly advancing technology, Sandra put her writing on hold to pursue a career in computer programming. After college, she worked as a systems support analyst for one of the largest wholesale distributing companies in North America. She later joined an educational software development firm as a trainer, where she discovered how much she enjoyed helping and teaching others.

In 1994, Sandra's passion for sailing took her to the Caribbean where she worked for a prominent yacht charter company for nearly four years before returning home to Vancouver. After realizing that the pleasures of the world did not fill the emptiness she felt, she found a love like no other in a relationship with Jesus Christ.

In 2002 Sandra left the corporate world once again, to enroll in Youth With A Mission's six-month Discipleship Training School in Kona, Hawaii. After completing the two-month missions field assignment portion of the course in the Philippines, she returned to Canada with a new heart for missions and a desire to teach others about the life-changing power of Jesus' love.

Today Sandra is once again finding inspiration at the 'typewriter' in between her duties as an administrative assistant and Children's Ministry leader. Surrounded by picturesque mountains and the waters of the Pacific, she makes her home in beautiful British Columbia, Canada.

To learn more about Sandra or to contact
her, visit www.sandracrawford.com.